LEARNING
from Working

A Guide for Cooperative Education/Internship Students

Joseph E. Barbeau, Ed.D.
Dean of Career Development & Placement
Director, Cooperative Education Research Center
Northeastern University
Boston, Massachusetts

William A. Stull, Ed.D.
Professor, Business & Marketing Education
College of Business
Utah State University
Logan, Utah

CA40AB
PUBLISHED BY
SOUTH-WESTERN PUBLISHING CO.
CINCINNATI, OH   WEST CHICAGO, IL   DALLAS, TX   LIVERMORE, CA

Copyright © 1990
by SOUTH-WESTERN PUBLISHING CO.
Cincinnati, Ohio

ISBN: 0-538-70102-1
Library of Congress Catalog Card Number: 88-63355
3 4 5 6 7 8 9 H 7 6 5 4
Printed in the United States of America

PREFACE

This Guide was written to assist two- and four-year college students participating in Cooperative Education or Internship programs in maximizing their learning opportunities. The learning that takes place as part of this off-campus experience is essential to the success of these programs. The activities in this Guide focus on preparing for, participating in, and utilizing the experiences available through working while attending college. As the late Herman Schneider, founder of cooperative education in 1906, has written, "There are aspects of every profession that cannot be learned in the classroom but must be learned where that profession is practiced. . . . Judgment based upon experience must supplement theory."[1] The authors believe that the learning that results from work does not happen just by working. It must be nurtured and enhanced. And that is the reason we have written this text.

The topics are organized in a chronological sequence following a typical pattern of student progression through the program. Section 1, Planning for the Experience, contains activities designed to assist students in developing profiles of themselves and their needs for experiential learning. In Section 2, Preparing for the Experience, the student is taught career skills such as job-search techniques, résumé preparation, cover-letter design, and interviewing techniques.

Section 3, Developing Your Training Program to Maximize Benefits, assists students in analyzing the job environment and employers' expectations. This information is then coupled with developing performance objectives for the work site and acquiring work-adjustment skills. All of the activities in Section 3 are aimed at producing the maximum benefit from the cooperative education/internship experience.

In the logical sequence of events, cooperative education/internship students next need to understand and utilize evaluation skills. Consequently, the activities in Section 4, Evaluating Your Job Progress, are designed to teach the evaluation process and its purpose in a work-experience program. Finally, students are taught to use skills acquired in the other sections to make the transition to permanent employment after graduation. Section 5, therefore, contains activities on maximizing promotion potential, understanding the need for further education, changing jobs, and developing a personal marketing plan. This section concludes with an evaluation of the total cooperative education/internship program. Each section contains a reference list for further reading.

Each activity begins with a specific statement of purpose for that activity, a brief introduction to the activity, and one or more hands-on assignments. These assignments require students to verbalize and internalize the materials being presented. Checklists, questions and answers, and brief paragraph responses are the principle methods used. This Guide is intended to be used for instruction—*not* merely read for information. Important or interesting points are often set off from the text.

A Program Manager's Guide is available for the teacher and/or program coordinator. This Guide contains suggestions on using the activities in either a seminar mode or as an individual instructional tool. Many of the activities can be expanded for classroom discussion. At the same time, this Guide can be used by the coordinator to counsel individual students.

---

[1] Herman Schneider, "Notes on the Co-op System," *The Proceedings of the Society for the Promotion of Engineering Education,* Vol. 18, 1910, p. 395.

Both authors are well known in cooperative and experiential education, have taught both undergraduate and graduate classes in cooperative education, and have directed doctoral dissertation research. Each has served as a consultant to many two- and four-year colleges in the United States. Between them they have nearly 50 years experience with cooperative education. Dr. William A. Stull is a Professor at Utah State University in Logan, Utah. He has many years of involvement with Cooperative Education and Marketing Education. He has conducted research in cooperative education and has written texts in marketing and in coordinating high school, community college, and university cooperative programs. Dr. Stull is active in the Cooperative Education Association and has attended many international and world conferences on cooperative education. He has written journal articles and research reports on various aspects of collegiate cooperative education programs.

Dr. Joseph E. Barbeau is Dean of Career Development and Placement at Northeastern University in Boston and Director of the Cooperative Education Research Center. He has been a cooperative education student, an employer of co-op students, a co-op coordinator, a co-op faculty member, and an administrator. Dr. Barbeau has conducted training seminars and workshops in 37 states and Canada for the past 15 years. He has written two books on Cooperative Education and numerous journal articles. He is active in the Cooperative Education Association and several of the state and regional co-op associations. Dr. Barbeau was the recipient of the 1989 Herman Schneider Award. This award was presented by the Cooperative Education Association for outstanding contributions to the advancement of the philosophy and practice of cooperative education.

The authors combine a breadth and depth of experience in cooperative eduction that assists the student in making the cooperative education or internship experience program a truly educational one.

CONTENTS

Contents

SECTION 1

Planning for the Experience

You have probably chosen to participate in the cooperative education/internship program for several specific reasons. Usually, one of these reasons relates to a need for practical experience that cannot be obtained in the classroom—a need that can be addressed only in the marketplace where certain skills are practiced. However, work that is not planned or is haphazardly chosen can interfere with your need to acquire specific skills that are important to you and to your career. Making decisions about your future is much smarter than just leaving things to chance.

In order to maximize the learning that will occur in this program, you must have some clear idea of what you want to accomplish with this cooperative education/internship experience and what skills you wish to develop. To ensure that the experience will produce the benefits you desire, you will need to do some planning before you start looking at specific opportunities.

In Section 1, several activities are designed to assist you in examining your values, personality, and interests. You will use this information, along with some assessment of your transferable skills, to develop a personal profile. Next you will determine the kind of skills and background information you need, in addition to what you already have, and where these experiences might be found. Methods of obtaining accurate career information and opportunities for making realistic career decisions will also be presented.

To supplement the information presented in the activities, a list of helpful resources is also provided. If your institution has a career resource center or a career library, some of these materials may be available there. Many of the suggested materials are obtainable in your college bookstore or other bookstores, some quite inexpensively. Armed with this information, you will be ready to begin your search for the *best* cooperative education/internship experience for you.

ACTIVITY 1
Developing Your Personal Profile

Purpose: To understand how your values, personality, interests, and skills can be used to develop a profile of yourself for presentation to a prospective employer.

In preparing for your cooperative education/internship experience, the first step is knowing who you are, what activities you like or dislike, and what skills you have that might interest an employer. Accordingly, you need to examine those aspects of your life carefully and honestly, keeping records for later reference. This step, broadly referred to as self-assessment, will include several activities designed to help you understand yourself.

There are many assessment instruments and activities available commercially, some of which must be mailed to the vendor for machine scoring. In this book you will receive immediate feedback for most activities. However, the use of other types of assessment will be discussed.

One of the early techniques designed to identify interests was the *Self-Directed Search* (SDS).[1] Developed by John Holland and marketed by Consulting Psychologists Press, it is self-administered, self-scored, and self-interpreted. Its purpose is to assist you in making appropriate career choices. Its usefulness has been proven over time, and the principles elaborated by Holland form the foundation for many newer assessment instruments.

More recently, Harrington and O'Shea have developed a similar instrument called the *Career Decision-Making* (CDM) *System*.[2] Using Holland's six personality types (with slightly different names), they have produced a self-assessment system that focuses on interests, skills, and values and uses this information to suggest possible career choices and job titles.

At the heart of both systems are six personality types. Your scores on either instrument allow you to determine your first, second, and third most appropriate career clusters. These personality types, with some descriptive adjectives, are listed here:

SDS	CDM	Descriptive Adjectives
Realistic	Crafts	Confirming, persistent, practical, direct, steady, honest, materialistic, shy
Investigative	Scientific	Curious, critical, precise, analytical, methodological, studious, intellectual, independent
Artistic	The Arts	Idealistic, imaginative, expressive, independent, intuitive, emotional, unconventional, impulsive
Social	Social	Cooperative, friendly, sociable, tactful, caring, responsible, generous, helpful

---

[1] John Holland, *Self-Directed Search* (Psychological Assessment Resources, Inc., 1987).

[2] T. F. Harrington and A. J. O'Shea, *Career Decision-Making System* (Circle Pines, Minn.: American Guidance Service, 1984).

SDS	CDM	Descriptive Adjectives
Enterprising	Business	Adventurous, energetic, ambitious, self-confident, persuasive, optimistic, talkative, domineering
Conventional	Clerical	Orderly, organized, obedient, conforming, conservative, efficient, persistent, conscientious

You can probably think of people you know who fit these categories. Your personality definitely affects your career choices. If you are not outgoing or verbally persuasive and do not like people, you probably will not succeed as a salesperson. Different personality characteristics are needed in different types of occupations.

In the same manner, our personal and work values, our skills, and our interests affect our career success. Getting to know yourself is the task of this first activity.

ASSESSING PERSONAL AND WORK VALUES

It may seem like a waste of time to answer questions about yourself and your values. You are probably saying, "Why do I need to do this? I know myself pretty well." Do you? Do you really see yourself as others see you? If you had to choose between two attractive job offers, how would you decide? Which offers the greater opportunity to satisfy a larger number of values? What are your values? Do you know what a value is? These and other questions need to be answered before you can proceed to examine the right career choices for you.

If you had to decide between jobs that allowed you to satisfy some of your work values and not others, which would you choose? To gain a better understanding of your own work values, please complete the following exercises:

1. Rank-order the ten work values that follow. Number 1 is the most important to you and number 10 is the least important. **No ties, please.**

Rank	Work Value
_____	Good salary
_____	Flexible schedule
_____	Independence
_____	Favorable geographic location
_____	Job security
_____	Opportunity for personal growth
_____	Intellectual stimulation
_____	Friendly co-workers
_____	Opportunity to travel
_____	Attractive benefit package

2. Now go over the list you have ranked and eliminate two of the values you could live without if you had to. Cross them off your list.

3. Once more, go over your list. In place of the two eliminated items, insert any two additional work values that are important to you. Renumber your list.

There are many more work values than those listed here. The two you added are examples of some that were not listed. However, the process is what is important. Some things are very important to us, and in the absence of those conditions we are not going to be happy in our work. Likewise, some things are not so important and can be sacrificed without any real loss.

1. Were you surprised at your rank order? Why?

2. Where did "good salary" rate? How do you feel about that? How did you define "good salary" in your own mind?

Now that you have examined values that are important in the work environment, it is time to look at some of your personal values. The following exercise will help you clarify values that are important to you in your personal life.

1. On the following list, rank the personal values in order of importance to you. Once again, 1 is the most important and 10 is the least important.

Rank	Personal Value
_____	Good health
_____	Respect from my peers
_____	Marriage and family
_____	Freedom to do what I want
_____	Adequate finances
_____	Living in a nice neighborhood
_____	Enough leisure time
_____	Opportunity for physical activity
_____	Opportunity for volunteer activities
_____	Time to be creative

2. What did you learn about your inventory of personal values?

3. What values would you have added that are not on the list?

Section 1   Planning for the Experience

4. Do you know what a value is now? If not, look it up in a dictionary or other reference book. Write your definition of a value here.

Now that you have clarified both your work values and your personal values, you can use this information to make discriminating career choices.

Please write a brief paragraph explaining how this knowledge of your personal and work values might affect your career decisions.

EXAMINING PERSONALITY AND INTERESTS

Another aspect of your profile is your personality and how your interests are shaped by personality. How would you describe yourself? In the space below, prepare a one-paragraph description of yourself. What are you really like? How do others see you?

Go back to the discussion of personality characteristics, SDS, and CDM in the first section of this activity. The far right-hand column is labeled "Descriptive Adjectives." Looking only at this column, circle those adjectives that describe some aspect of your personality.

1. Using either the SDS *or* CDM column, identify which SDS or CDM category has the greatest number of adjectives circled? _____

2. Which category is second? _____ third? _____

3. How would you describe your personality? (for example, Business–Social–Crafts)

_____   _____   _____
            first   second   third

In Activity 20, Making the Transition to Permanent Employment, you will see how your values and personal characteristics may affect your career choices and job satisfaction. Save the exercises in this activity so that you can review them when you complete Activity 20.

DETERMINING TRANSFERABLE SKILLS

Do you possess any skills that you can describe to an employer? Of course you do. But which ones? Do you know what your skills are? What are transferable skills? Answering these questions will be the purpose of this last section in Activity 1. Again, there are several commercially available instruments to help you find out, one of which is *The New Quick Job-Hunting Map*.[3] For an in-depth understanding of your skills, this technique, developed by Richard Bolles, is excellent and well worth the time it takes to complete. For purposes of this text, you will survey your skills through a series of questions.

What skills do you possess? Remember, how you acquired the skill is not important. Skills are acquired not only in job situations but in other settings, such as hobbies, leisure activities, and volunteer work. Skills that carry over from one situation to another are referred to as **transferable skills.**

What skills have you used? In the following list, put a 1, 2, or 3 beside those skills that you possess (1 = minimal skill, 2 = moderate level of skill, 3 = good level of competence).

_____ 1. Visualizing shapes and forms

_____ 2. Reducing or enlarging drawings

_____ 3. Drawing basic mechanical designs

_____ 4. Solving geometric problems

_____ 5. Seeing relationships between different-size objects

_____ 6. Measuring sizes and shapes

_____ 7. Drawing freehand

_____ 8. Using color in design

_____ 9. Matching and blending colors

_____ 10. Designing artistic creations

_____ 11. Decorating rooms and objects

_____ 12. Painting with oils, acrylics, or watercolors

_____ 13. Playing a musical instrument

_____ 14. Singing in public

_____ 15. Reading music

_____ 16. Writing music

_____ 17. Dancing in groups

_____ 18. Arranging musical compositions

_____ 19. Writing short stories, poems, plays, or other literary works

_____ 20. Writing clear and concise reports

_____ 21. Speaking before groups

_____ 22. Debating or giving dramatic performances

_____ 23. Correcting written documents

_____ 24. Translating foreign languages

---

[3] Richard Bolles, *The New Quick Job-Hunting Map* (Berkeley, Calif.: Ten Speed Press, 1985).

_____ 25. Organizing ideas and people

_____ 26. Leading groups

_____ 27. Working with others to get tasks done

_____ 28. Initiating group activities

_____ 29. Delegating responsibility

_____ 30. Listening to others

_____ 31. Coaching or tutoring others

_____ 32. Giving instructions

_____ 33. Selling products and services

_____ 34. Advising others on problems

_____ 35. Influencing decisions

_____ 36. Motivating group members

_____ 37. Solving number problems

_____ 38. Budgeting expenses

_____ 39. Computing mathematical problems

_____ 40. Calculating income taxes

_____ 41. Tabulating data

_____ 42. Using the computer for data manipulation

_____ 43. Repairing mechanical or electrical equipment

_____ 44. Carving, woodworking, sewing, knitting, etc.

_____ 45. Setting up mechanical or electrical equipment

_____ 46. Using tools and implements in hobby and/or work

_____ 47. Typing or using business machines

_____ 48. Making objects for arts and crafts

_____ 49. Using knowledge to solve problems

_____ 50. Examining data to understand relationships

_____ 51. Conducting scientific experiments

_____ 52. Using computer or video games

_____ 53. Investigating possible solutions

_____ 54. Designing new approaches to solve existing problems

Add your scores as follows:

Questions 1–6	Total	_____
Questions 7–12		_____
Questions 13–18		_____
Questions 19–24		_____
Questions 25–30		_____

Questions 31–36   _____

Questions 37–42   _____

Questions 43–48   _____

Questions 49–54   _____

What was your highest score for any six-question group? _____

Second highest?   Lowest?

_____   _____

Questions 1–6 deal with spatial relationships; 7–12 relate to artistic ability; 13–18 assess your musical skill; 19–24 relate to your writing and use of language; 25–30 relate to your need to socialize and to influence others; 31–36 indicate your ability in the helping arena; 37–42 reflect your skill with numbers; 43–48 relate to your manual and mechanical skills; and 49–54 examine your general problem-solving skills.

In which group was your score highest? _____

What group was second? _____

What skill area was your weakest? _____

Write a paragraph answering these questions:

What did you learn about your skills? Which skills would you prefer to use? Which skill areas do you need to develop further? Why?

Can any of these skills be developed through the use of cooperative education/internship assignments? Describe the kind of assignment that might help you to improve your skills.

ACTIVITY 2
Examining Your Career Direction

Purpose: To help you make career decisions and to assist you in discovering gaps in your experience.

Your cooperative education/internship assignment can provide a great deal of career information if you are ready to use the placement as such a resource. First you must make some tentative decisions about your initial career choices so that some sense of direction is possible. Remember, this career choice is *not* a lifetime career. It is probable that you will have as many as six completely different careers (and possibly as many as twenty different jobs) by the time you retire.

IDENTIFYING THE EXPERIENCE GAPS

Having made a tentative career choice, you need to examine your experience in light of the skills identified in Activity 1. In preparing for an initial career choice, you can then see where there are gaps in your experience. Once these gaps have been identified, the cooperative education/internship assignment can be planned to fill some of them. What do you think? Are you ready to make some initial decisions? It is not as difficult as it might seem.

To keep this task manageable, try not to think in terms of a lifetime career but look at what some of your options will be after you finish this program. The questions that follow will assist in this process.

1. Why did you choose the program and school in which you are enrolled?

2. When you decided to pursue this program of study, what did you think would be your first job after graduating?

3. Do you have plans to advance in this career field? If so, what do you now see as your ultimate goal in this field?

4. Knowing what you do about this initial occupation, you have decided that additional schooling is necessary. However, not all the training you need will come from classwork. What kinds of

additional experience do you feel must be added to those experiences that you have already had?

5. What transferable skills must you still acquire?

6. In what kinds of businesses can these skills be acquired?

7. Do you need to develop or improve your affective skills? **Affective skills** are those that involve attitudes, behaviors, and professional manner, as opposed to technical or content-oriented skills. List the affective skills that you need to improve.

_____   _____

_____   _____

_____   _____

_____   _____

FILLING IN THE EXPERIENCE GAPS

Now that you have taken an objective look at yourself, you should determine the type of cooperative education/internship assignments most beneficial to you.

If you and your career counselor or coordinator have discussed the types of experiences available in the cooperative education/internship program, answer Question 1. (Use a separate sheet of paper.)

If you have not discussed possible assignments with your career counselor, answer Question 2. (Use a separate sheet of paper.)

1. Given the cooperative education/internship assignments available, which of your skills can be acquired or further developed by each of your possible assignments?

2. List the types of assignments that you would like, assuming they were available. Focus on which skills could be developed.

ACTIVITY 3
Using Career Information

Purpose: To use resources of up-to-date career information and to identify organizations that can provide the kinds of experiences you need.

Now that you have identified some of your interests and skills and have determined an initial career direction, it is time to find out what additional skills you need and where you can obtain them. This career information can help you to make informed choices regarding the most appropriate cooperative education/internship assignment for you.

There are several ways to attack this problem. You could just accept any kind of assignment and hope that some of the experiences you need will be available. This is a rather haphazard approach and, without considerable luck, could waste a great deal of time and energy. Another approach would be to describe your interests and needs in great detail to your career counselor and let him or her provide the appropriate assignment. This arrangement may be ideal but is probably impractical unless your counselor has a very small student load and a great deal of time. So what can you do? You can prepare yourself to take the best advantage of the marketplace by doing some of the work yourself. This activity should help you get started.

USING THE INFORMATIONAL INTERVIEW

One effective way of obtaining career information is the **informational interview.** This is *not* a job interview, but rather, an interview with a person who is involved in some aspect of a career in which you have an interest. Keep in mind the fact that the information is current and comes directly from someone working in the field. Interviewees can be neighbors, acquaintances, alumni of your school, or any professional working in the appropriate field. Generally, they should work in a position in which you are interested or at least be familiar with that position.

Conducting an informational interview is not complicated or threatening. Since you are not being evaluated during the interview, it should be fairly easy. Check your career resource center or placement office; some institutions offer a videotape that describes the informational interview. Viewing a tape may help you to feel more comfortable with the interview process.

To arrange for an informational interview, call the person selected and request an interview. Make sure this person understands that you are *not* interviewing for a job but that you are looking for career information.

For this assignment, choose a career or occupation that interests you, find an appropriate person to interview, and conduct an informational interview. Here is a list of questions that you should ask during the interview. Remember, you want *information,* so let the person being interviewed do most of the talking. After your interview has been completed, please answer these questions with the responses of the *person you interviewed.*

1. What skills, education, and training are needed for this position?

2. What are the special requirements of this job?

3. How did you acquire the skills and training needed for this position?

4. Are there other ways of obtaining the same skills and training? How?

5. Where do you have to go (geographic location) to get this experience? How much time would it take to complete these requirements? What are the approximate costs?

6. Describe a typical workday. (You may wish to use a separate piece of paper for this answer.)

7. What aspects of this work appeal to you? Why?

8. What aspects of this work do not appeal to you? What can you do about it?

After you have analyzed the information collected during the informational interview, please give *your* responses to the following questions.

1. Are you still interested in this occupation?

   Yes _____   No _____   Still not sure _____

2. What aspects of the job appeal to you?

3. Which do not appeal to you?

4. What career or occupation did you select for this assignment?

   _____

5. Whom did you interview?

   Name _____

   Position _____

   Organization _____

USING PLACEMENT OFFICE FILES AND OCCUPATIONAL INFORMATION

Many placement offices maintain files on the organizations with which they work, including those that recruit on campus. Typically, the files contain such information as annual reports, descriptive brochures, organizational charts, descriptions of products and/or services, and locations of various operations. Some may be complete and others very sketchy. Usually it's possible to find out a great deal about a specific organization and its products or services.

The placement office or career center should also have some printed materials that deal with occupations and career clusters, as well as directories of various kinds. Resources such as the *Occupational Outlook Handbook,* the *Dictionary of Occupational Titles,* and the *Guide to Occupational Exploration* are standard in most such offices. Those with greater resources will have such additional materials as the *Vocational Biographies Series,* the *VGM Career Horizons Series,* and *Peterson's Guides,* just to name a few. Check to see what is available at your institution. Sometimes these materials are also available in the reference room of your college library.

Some two- and four-year colleges have a computerized career information system available. There are many different types in use, and some provide more information than others. Usually these systems contain information on a variety of occupations and may include tools for self-assessment as well. If such a system is available on your campus, you might want to verify your informational interview information with this computerized information. You may also want to check it against the print resources. It is always important to compare information from several sources.

Some things to consider when collecting career information include the following:

- How accurate is the information?
- How current is the information?
- How complete is the information?
- How biased is the information?

Your assignment is to select an occupation in which you have some interest. Locate at least *three* print resources that contain information about this occupation and write a paragraph about each one. List the types of important information found in each source and the kinds of information you felt were still missing. Be sensitive to stereotypes that are likely to be present in some sources. Watch for stereotypes relating to sex, race, age, religion, or social class. Remember, there are many sources of career information: your teachers, local libraries, relatives, your academic department library, local businesspeople, neighbors, and counselors. Use them all. (Use a separate piece of paper for this assignment.)

ADDITIONAL RESOURCES

Bolles, Richard N. *The New Quick Job Hunting Map*. Berkeley, Calif.: Ten Speed Press, 1985.
Bolles, Richard N. *The 1988 What Color Is Your Parachute? A Practical Manual for Job Hunters and Career Changers*. Berkeley, Calif.: Ten Speed Press, 1988.
Figler, H. *The Complete Job Search Handbook*. New York: Holt, Rinehart & Winston, 1987.
Harrington, T. F., and A. J. O'Shea. *Career Decision-Making System*. Circle Pines, Minn.: American Guidance Service, 1982.
Harrington, T. F., and A. J. O'Shea, eds. *Guide for Occupational Exploration*. Circle Pines, Minn.: American Guidance Service, 1984.
Holland, John. *Self-Directed Search*. Palo Alto, Calif.: Consulting Psychologists Press, undated.
Kirschenbaum, H. *Advanced Values Clarification*. La Jolla, Calif.: University Associates, 1977.
Peterson's Guides. Princeton, N.J.: Peterson's Guides, annually.
U.S. Bureau of Labor Statistics. *Occupational Projections and Training Data*. A Statistical and Research Supplement to the 1986–87 *Occupational Outlook Handbook*. Washington, D.C.: U.S. Department of Labor, 1986.
U.S. Bureau of Labor Statistics. *Occupational Outlook Handbook*. Washington, D.C.: U.S. Department of Labor, 1987.
U.S. Bureau of Labor Statistics. *Occupational Outlook Quarterly*. Washington, D.C.: U.S. Department of Labor, quarterly.
U.S. Department of Labor, *Dictionary of Occupational Titles*. 4th ed. Washington, D.C.: U.S. Government Printing Office, 1977.
VGM Career Horizons Series. Lincolnwood, Ill.: VGM Career Horizons, various publication dates.
Vocational Biographies Series. Sauk Centre, Minn.: Vocational Biographies, various years.

SECTION 2

Preparing for the Experience

Preparing for your cooperative education/internship assignment is an important step in moving from the college campus to the world of work. One of the purposes of your college's cooperative education/internship program is to assist you in this process. This section begins with an activity that asks you to explore the nature and purposes of your college's cooperative education/internship program. You will find out in this activity how your program operates and how you can become involved.

After exploring your program, you will complete a series of activities designed to help you find and secure a meaningful cooperative education/internship work assignment. In Activity 5 you will learn how to find potential job leads, what to do with these leads, and how to prepare a prospecting letter that will help you obtain a job interview. Activity 6 provides you with step-by-step development of a résumé that will highlight your educational background and work experience. This activity also shows you how to prepare a cover letter to send along with your résumé to prospective employers.

In Activity 7 you will be exposed to specific suggestions and guidelines to follow in completing job application forms accurately and completely. Also included in this activity are examples of typical letters used in the employment process. Activity 8 relates to employment testing and legal aspects of the employment process from the job seeker's point of view.

This section concludes with two important activities that relate to the job interview process. Activity 9 provides recommendations and activities that will help you prepare for the interview. The last activity will give you an opportunity to practice and refine your actual interview skills.

ACTIVITY 4
Understanding the Nature and Purposes of Your Cooperative Education/Internship Program

Purpose: To increase your awareness of the nature, purposes, and advantages of your college's cooperative education/internship program. To help you determine how this educational strategy will assist you in reaching your educational and career goals.

Cooperative education/internship programs are not new. In 1906 the concept was introduced in engineering at the University of Cincinnati. The cooperative plan called for the integration of periods of related work experience with periods of academic study. One section of students worked in industry while the other attended regular college classes. Then, at a specified time, the students in the two sections would change places. Multiple industry-based experiences became more advanced in job sophistication as students advanced in their studies. At that time the main benefit seen by business and industry was that graduates of the cooperative system would be better prepared to be productive immediately upon graduation. They would have a taste of the real world of work, understand state-of-the-art technology, and be ready to become functioning members of an industry work team.

Today the cooperative education/internship concept has been embraced by more than 1000 colleges and universities. More than 200,000 college students each year benefit from participation in programs that combine supervised work experience with college study. Some programs alternate periods of full-time work with periods of full-time study. Others offer a parallel program whereby students work and attend school concurrently. Still others provide cooperative education/internship positions in the summer. The idea of integrating work and study has spread to practically all disciplines on college campuses—from those with technical orientations, such as engineering and computer science, to business, and more recently to the social sciences and liberal arts.

USEFUL PROGRAM TERMINOLOGY

Like most other fields and specialized activities, cooperative education/internship programs employ their own terminology. Your understanding of the following terms will be helpful to you as you complete the remainder of this activity.

Cooperative Education/Internship Program—Cooperative education/internship students have an opportunity to blend theory and practice. Students mix periods of full- or part-time study with periods of full- and part-time career-related work experience.

Parallel Plan—Cooperative education/internship students attend college and work concurrently on a part-time basis during the academic semester or quarter.

Alternating Plan—Cooperative education/internship students alternate semesters or quarters of full-time study with quarters of full-time work experience.

Cooperative Education/Internship Director—The person on college campuses who has the overall responsibility for the scope and direction of the college's cooperative education program.

Cooperative Education/Internship Coordinators—Professional staff members who work directly with the placement of students in cooperative education/internship assignments and coordinate these students throughout the duration of the program.

Job or Work Assignment—The specific tasks assigned to students who are working on cooperative education/internship work periods.

BENEFITS OF PARTICIPATION

Regardless of the pattern of organization that your college follows in its cooperative education/internship program, your participation offers you many benefits. These are some of the most frequently mentioned advantages:

- The classes you take in your college major will have more meaning because you will be able to apply what you are learning.
- You gain a head start in beginning your career and securing permanent employment upon graduation. Many co-op/internship students nationally are offered full-time employment by their co-op employers.
- You earn money to meet your college expenses.
- You gain practical experience and are exposed to the latest of technology and equipment used in the workplace.
- You learn job-seeking and job-holding skills. You gain maturity, professionalism, and self-confidence.
- You have an opportunity to sample your chosen career field early in your educational program.
- In the long run you will earn more money and advance more rapidly in your chosen career field.

PROGRAM ORGANIZATION AND CURRENT STATUS ON YOUR CAMPUS

Cooperative education/internship programs are organized differently on different campuses. To gain a better understanding of how your college's cooperative education/internship program is organized, please answer the following questions.

1. What is the exact title of your college's program?

    _____

2. Who is responsible for supervising or directing this program?

    _____

3. Where on your campus is the main office located for this activity?

    Name of building: _____

    Room number: _____

    Telephone number: _____

4. How many students are currently involved in this program on your college campus?

    _____

5. What programs or curricula on your campus provide an opportunity for students to become involved in cooperative education/internship activities? Please list by program or major title.

    _____   _____

    _____   _____

    _____   _____

    _____   _____

    _____

6. What are the requirements for enrollment and participation in this program for your particular college major?

Year in college required for participation: _____

Grade point average: _____

Other requirements (please list): _____

7. How much time would you be required to spend on a work assignment if you were to elect to participate in this program?

Hours per week; quarters, semesters: _____

8. Do cooperative education/internship work assignments earn academic credits for your participation?

Yes _____   No _____

Minimum number of credits: _____

Maximum number of credits: _____

9. In your own words explain how this program operates on your campus.

10. Is there an official application form you must fill out before you can participate in the program?

Yes _____   No _____

If yes, obtain a copy of the application form from the cooperative/internship office.

11. If you were interested in participating in the program, what steps should you take to become involved?

FACULTY OPINION

College faculty are generally very supportive of the cooperative education/internship concept. They enjoy having students in their classes who have practical experience in their field.

Interview a faculty member in your academic field or major department. Ask what he or she sees as the major advantages and disadvantages of your participation in the college's cooperative education/internship program.

1. What does this person see as the major advantages? List three.

2. What does this person see as the major disadvantages? List three.

3. Ask the faculty member to explain his or her role in your cooperative education/internship experience. In the space provided, summarize how he or she would be involved.

4. How does the faculty member feel that the cooperative education/internship program will help you to reach your educational and career goals?

COOPERATIVE EDUCATION/INTERNSHIP STAFF OPINION

Many colleges and universities have a centralized staff that works with cooperative education/internship activities. Most cooperative education directors have had a great deal of experience in helping students make realistic educational plans and career goals. Naturally they are interested in having students enroll in cooperative/internship programs, but only if that appears to be the right choice for the student.

Interview the cooperative education/internship director or a program coordinator to learn what he or she sees as the major advantages and disadvantages of your participation in the college's cooperative education/internship program.

1. What does this person see as the major advantages? List three.

2. What does this person see as the major disadvantages? List three.

3. How does this person feel that the cooperative education/internship program will help you to further your educational and career goals?

YOUR EXPECTATIONS FOR THE PROGRAM

Students who choose to participate in a cooperative education/internship program enter with certain expectations, which may or may not be completely realistic. In the space provided, identify the benefits you expect from your participation. Then review your ideas with the cooperative education/internship director, one of the coordinators, or a faculty member involved in the program.

ACTIVITY 5
Locating and Contacting Prospective Employers

Purpose: To develop a list of prospective employers and to make effective contacts that will result in an interview.

Before you can realize the benefits of additional work experiences, you must make contact with employers that can provide the kinds of assignments you desire. In some cases, your cooperative education/internship coordinator will do the job development for you and present you with a list of options. All you need do, then, is to choose the appropriate one.

What happens, though, when the type of experience you seek is not available in one of these options? What should you do if you need to develop your own placement opportunities? Many cooperative education/internship programs expect students either to participate jointly with the co-op coordinator in the job search process or to do it all themselves. In that case, you will need to proceed as outlined in this activity.

To locate and contact prospective employers, you must follow certain steps:

1. Develop a list of prospective firms for the type of experience you seek. This does not mean that these organizations have openings or are interested in hiring you. That determination comes later. To begin, you need a list of *all* possibilities within your geographical limits.
2. Qualify these organizations. It is through this process that your list of "suspects" becomes refined and shortened to a real list of "prospects."
3. Identify the appropriate decision maker in each organization. This is the person whom you will contact by exploratory letter or by telephone. The content of such a letter and a discussion of effective telephone techniques are presented later in this activity.
4. Follow up on these contacts without being an annoyance and without alienating your contact.

The way in which you develop your list and make your contact may determine whether you get the interview you want.

DEVELOPING A PROSPECT LIST

After identifying gaps in your experience (Activity 2) and learning how to obtain career information (Activity 3), you are ready to put this knowledge to use. You will develop a list of potential employers that have the possibility of providing the kind of experience you need. This list should include any organization that might provide cooperative education/internship training. Later, the list will be refined.

Using several sheets of paper, begin now to list the names and addresses of every organization you can find that *could* provide the kind of experience you want. Avoid letting your thoughts channel into obvious paths only. Sometimes the job you seek might be in a less obvious setting. For example, if you are seeking experience in cost accounting, do not confine your search only to manufacturing firms. Remember that hospitals, human service agencies, and many other non-manufacturing operations have need for cost accountants.

Here are some ways you can find names of potential employers:

1. Read the classified ads in newspapers, in appropriate professional journals, and on the bulletin board in your college placement office.

2. Look in the Yellow Pages of your telephone directory.
3. Go to your career resource center, placement office, or library reference room and check some of the following publications:
   a. The *CPC Annual,* published by the College Placement Council.
   b. *Standard & Poor's Register of Corporations.*
   c. Dun & Bradstreet's *Million Dollar Directory.*
   d. *Moody's Manuals,* six in all, according to type of business.
   e. *Fortune 500,* published by *Fortune* magazine.
   f. *Thomas Register of American Manufacturers.*
   g. Various local listings, such as directories of local manufacturers, local Chamber of Commerce directories, local business directories, and your local State Employment Service office.

See if your institution has a career resource center or career library, which may have files on the various organizations that recruit on campus. You may find copies of annual reports, product or service brochures, and names of contact persons.

While doing this research, do not forget to talk to people. Your family, faculty members, neighbors, classmates, and friends, as well as business contacts, all have information about prospective employers. Keep expanding your list, but do not include those employers that obviously would not provide the kinds of experiences you seek. If in doubt, go ahead and include the organization at this point.

How is your list coming along? You should have several pages by now.

QUALIFYING PROSPECTS

Your list should now contain every organization you could possibly find that might offer the kind of experience you desire. Salespeople would refer to this list as "suspects," not "prospects"; that is, you suspect that these organizations might be helpful. Now it is time to edit your list, to eliminate those "suspects" that really cannot help you. The remaining "short list" will consist of your prospects. This is where research on organizations pays off.

Which organizations are hiring in areas that can provide you with your needed experience? To find out, you must examine the classified ads closely. You will also need to review annual reports and read the local business news. Above all, you should talk to people who might know what these organizations do. It is possible that you will want to telephone someone in the organization and ask questions. Next to each name and address on your list, make a note that indicates to you what your research shows. A notation system may help. For example, "Y" means "Yes, this organization probably would hire someone to do what I want to do." "N" means "No, it is unlikely that this organization can provide the kind of experience I am seeking." "?" means "I don't know. At this time my research does not allow me to answer the question." You may prefer to use a numbering system in which 1 means "very likely," 2 means "possibly has the positions I seek," 3 means "doubtful," and 4 means "unlikely." You can then contact organizations on the "1" list first.

IDENTIFYING THE DECISION MAKER

Once you have your list of prospects (even if it represents only your best guesses), you need to know the name of the appropriate person to contact in each organization. This person must be the decision maker and must be the one who hires people for the position you seek. It must be the person who makes the budgetary decisions regarding the phase of the operation in which you wish to work. Salespeople have a simple way of identifying the decision maker. They never accept a "no" answer from someone who is not in a position to say yes. If the decision is not within someone's scope of responsibility, the person can always say no. Only the decision maker can say either yes *or* no.

The simplest way to get this information is to ask. Telephone the organization and ask the operator, receptionist, or secretary who answers for the name of the appropriate person to answer questions regarding your area of interest. In the vast majority of cases, the individual's name and title will be provided. Be sure to get the correct spelling of the name. If you are unsure, ask the person to repeat it or spell it for you. Nothing makes a worse impression on a prospective employer than to receive a letter with his or her name spelled incorrectly. Add these names, titles, and phone numbers to your prospect list.

PREPARING THE EXPLORATORY LETTER

The **exploratory letter** is the cover letter that will accompany your résumé when you request an employment interview. In many cases, you will not be responding to an advertisement or other invitation to apply. You are trying to develop a cooperative education/internship assignment with the organization, and prospective employers usually do not advertise positions of that sort.

Your letter must accomplish four purposes and not exceed one page in doing so. It must (1) introduce you to the prospective employer, (2) describe the kind of experience or opportunity you seek, (3) attach some benefit to your employment, and (4) request an interview.

Introduce Yourself to the Prospective Employer

In introducing yourself to the employer, you want to highlight those skills that you feel would be most important to this particular employer. These skills will be amplified in your résumé, but your letter should direct the reader to them. The sample letter in Figure 5.1 emphasizes the appropriate courses and summer experiences, as well as the applicant's interest in the field.

Describe the Experience/Opportunity You Seek

In describing the kind of experience or opportunity you seek, try to be as specific as possible. It helps the employer if you can identify specific opportunities or positions in the organization. In Figure 5.1 the cooperative education student mentions the position of chemical technician in the metallurgy laboratory and expresses his desire to increase his skill with laboratory equipment used in metallurgy.

Attach Some Benefit to Your Employment

Permitting you to obtain the kind of experience you want is not enough incentive for an employer to hire you. You must also show that you can provide some kind of service to that employer while you are learning. Your previous skills, no matter how minimal, allow you to perform tasks that employers must hire people to accomplish. In Figure 5.1, "Harry Walker" indicates that he can perform certain tasks as a chemical technician. He has learned to use certain kinds of general laboratory equipment and has performed a variety of menial tasks in other industrial laboratories. He should be better prepared than a "new hire" without these skills, so he is trying to capitalize on his work history.

Request an Interview

Finally, our student states clearly his purpose for writing. He wants an appointment for an interview. In the third paragraph of the letter in Figure 5.1, he asks for an appointment and indicates what further steps he will take to arrange for the interview.

Notice that the exploratory letter uses a standard business letter format, including (1) return address and date, (2) inside address, (3) salutation, (4) body of the letter, and (5) complimentary close. These letter parts are labeled in Figure 5.2. The specific style and placement of these items on the page allows for some flexibility of choice. Figure 5.2 is only one example of how this might be done. You may use any appropriate letter style.

Notice also that the body of the letter contains a "thank you." When requesting this kind of consideration, you should express your appreciation in advance. The letter should be typewritten or printed by a computer, centered vertically on the page, have adequate margins on the right and left, be free of spelling and grammatical errors, and be neat. If it is produced by computer,

Figure 5.1 Sample Cover Letter

123 Fourth Street
Bowling Green, OH 43402-6721
February 28, 19--

Ms. Mary C. Gomez
Research Director
Useful Alloys Corporation
910 Eleventh Avenue
Hamilton, OH 45011-1963

Dear Ms. Gomez:

I am interested in a temporary position as a chemical
technician in your metallurgy laboratory. On my enclosed
resume you will note that I have finished two years as a
chemistry major at Midwestern University, have completed
analytical chemistry, and have worked the past two summers
in an industrial chemical laboratory. My strong interest
in metallurgy, combined with my courses and my laboratory
experience, provide me with the background to make a
worthwhile contribution as chemical technician in your
organization.

For a project in analytical chemistry, I wrote a research
paper on the use of molybdenum in specialized steel
alloys. In my summer jobs, I learned how to use various
kinds of instrumentation to do assay analysis. The
specific instruments used are detailed on my resume.

I would like to make an appointment with you so that we
might explore the ways in which my cooperative education
program would allow me to make a contribution to your
company. As your employee, I would also be able to
increase my skill with laboratory equipment used in
metallurgy. I will telephone you within two weeks to
arrange for an interview at a mutually convenient time.

Thank you for your consideration. If you need additional
information, please contact me at (513) 555-2431.

Very truly yours,

Harry Walker

Harry Walker

Figure 5.2 Sample Cover Letter

return
address and ⎰ 123 Fourth Street
date line ⎱ Bowling Green, OH 43402-6721
⎱ February 28, 19--

Ms. Mary C. Gomez
Research Director   ⎱
Useful Alloys Corporation ⎰ inside
910 Eleventh Avenue   address
Hamilton, OH 45011-1963 ⎰

Dear Ms. Gomez:} salutation

I am interested in a temporary position as a chemical
technician in your metallurgy laboratory. On my enclosed
resume you will note that I have finished two years as a
chemistry major at Midwestern University, have completed
analytical chemistry, and have worked the past two summers
in an industrial chemical laboratory. My strong interest
in metallurgy, combined with my courses and my laboratory
experience, provide me with the background to make a
worthwhile contribution as chemical technician in your
organization.

For a project in analytical chemistry, I wrote a research
paper on the use of molybdenum in specialized steel
alloys. In my summer jobs, I learned how to use various
kinds of instrumentation to do assay analysis. The
specific instruments used are detailed on my resume.

I would like to make an appointment with you so that we
might explore the ways in which my cooperative education
program would allow me to make a contribution to your
company. As your employee, I would also be able to
increase my skill with laboratory equipment used in
metallurgy. I will telephone you within two weeks to
arrange for an interview at a mutually convenient time.

Thank you for your consideration. If you need additional
information, please contact me at (513) 555-2431.

complimentary close ⎰ Very truly yours,

signature ⎰ *Harry Walker*
typed name ⎱ Harry Walker

remember that the various automatic spelling programs may not use the correct word in context when two choices exist. Likewise, these programs do not flag errors in sentence structure. There is no substitute for careful proofreading.

If you type your letter on a typewriter, be sure that the type is clean, that the ribbon is dark enough for easy readability, and that the paper is opaque. You should not be able to read another page through the first one.

USING THE TELEPHONE EFFECTIVELY

When you call to arrange for your interview, the impression you make on the telephone is extremely important. In your first real contact with a prospective employer, you will be the voice on the other end of the wire. Think about it. When you receive a call from someone you have never met, do you try to form a mental picture of that person on the telephone? Most people do, and there is a good probability that the employer is doing it too. What kind of mental picture will you project? Are you articulate? Can you make yourself easily understood? Do your use of language and pronunciation stereotype you? Are you interesting and enthusiastic? Are you confident without being cocky? Are you assertive without being aggressive? Are you polite? Do you have a convincing message? The answers to these and other questions help form the mental picture of you. How do you look to someone on the other end of that wire?

Before calling, understand the purpose of your call and know how the call should proceed. Think about how you will introduce yourself. What is it you want from this employer? What can you offer in return for his or her decision to hire you? When are you available for an interview? Do you know how to get there? How will you find the person when you arrive?

Some of these items are the same ones that appear in the exploratory letter, and others have to do with confirming specific arrangements. Before hanging up, be sure that all necessary arrangements have been made and that you know how to contact the interviewer if something unexpected arises. It is equally important that the person be able to reach you if a change in plans becomes necessary. While doing all these things, remember to *be brief*. This is not the interview. You can provide greater detail at that time.

FOLLOWING UP ON CONTACTS

In the activities that follow, you will be learning to create a résumé, to complete application forms, and to conduct a successful interview. During this process, and after, you need to follow up on these contacts if there are lapses in communication. It is important that you keep in touch so that your opportunity doesn't fall through the cracks—that is, get lost through omission or oversight. If after a reasonable time you have had no further contact with an employer with whom you have unfinished business, you should initiate that contact. *Follow-up is your responsibility*. It may take the form of an additional letter or a phone call, but it is necessary. After the process is complete, it is appropriate for you to send a thank-you letter, expressing your appreciation for being considered. Samples of such letters are given in Figures 5.3 and 5.4.

Figure 5.3   Sample Follow-Up Letter

123 Fourth Street
Bowling Green, OH 43402-6721
March 27, 19--

Ms. Mary C. Gomez
Research Director
Useful Alloys Corporation
910 Eleventh Avenue
Hamilton, OH 45011-1963

Dear Ms. Gomez:

When we last talked on March 10, 1989, you indicated
that you would be in touch with me by March 20
regarding a chemical technician position. Not yet
having heard from you, I am wondering if there is
some further information you may need me to supply.

Please allow me to reemphasize my interest in your
organization and my willingness to answer any
remaining questions you may have. My daytime
telephone number is 555-8093.

Once again, thank you for your kind attention.

Very truly yours,

Harry Walker

Harry Walker

Figure 5.4 Sample Thank-You Letter

123 Fourth Street
Bowling Green, OH 43402-6721
April 1, 19--

Ms. Mary C. Gomez
Research Director
Useful Alloys Corporation
910 Eleventh Avenue
Hamilton, OH 45011-1963

Dear Ms. Gomez:

Thank you for the kindness shown to me when I was
interviewing with Useful Alloys Corporation. Because
of your willingness to place a cooperative education
student in one of your laboratories, I received an
offer of employment from Leslie Chase in your Steel
Alloys Fabrication Laboratory. I am looking forward
to beginning my association with your organization on
April 17.

Sincerely,

Harry Walker

Harry Walker

ACTIVITY 6
Building a High-Quality Résumé and Application Letter

Purpose: To provide you with information necessary to prepare a high-quality résumé for use in marketing yourself to prospective employers. To show you how to prepare a cover letter to send to employers along with your résumé.

One of the first steps in preparing for participation in your college's cooperative education/ internship program is to prepare a **résumé.** A résumé is a one- or two-page typewritten summary of important facts and information about you. It is your personal advertisement and is prepared in order to interest prospective employers in your qualifications. It briefly tells who you are, describes your employment objectives, summarizes your background and experience, identifies your references, and may contain other additional information.

The résumé serves a number of purposes:

1. A good résumé helps you gain confidence in yourself by making you more aware of what you have to offer employers.
2. A résumé shows employers that you are well organized, prepared, and serious about being employed.
3. A well-written résumé will help you in completing job application forms more accurately and easily.
4. Most important, it will help to interest employers in the possibility of interviewing you and offering you employment.

The résumé you prepare will usually be your first introduction to a prospective employer. Therefore, it must be designed to make a good first impression. Generally, employers use résumés to select the individuals they would like to interview. Since an employer usually spends *less than one minute* reviewing a résumé, the one you prepare must be brief, readable in format, visually pleasing, and absolutely free of any typographical or spelling errors. It is important for you to spend some extra time in developing your first professional résumé. Chances are fairly good that you will build on this same résumé in the future, rather than starting from scratch. For example, when you are ready to graduate and seek full-time employment, it will be a relatively easy task simply to update your résumé by adding the experience you have gained as a participant in the cooperative education/internship program.

RÉSUMÉ FORMATS

A number of different formats are used in résumé preparation. Two generally acceptable formats are the chronological and the functional. The **chronological résumé** shown in Figure 6.1 identifies your education and work experience in a reverse chronological order, listing your most recent degree and recent employment experience first. All the information you present is organized by date. Titles of positions held and names of employing organizations are prominent. Duties and accomplishments associated with each position and organization are listed immediately following.

Figure 6.1 Chronological Résumé

MARK SMITH	CAMPUS ADDRESS (until 6/1/89) 767 East 400 North #2 Logan, UT 84321 (801) 555-7522	HOME ADDRESS 2523 South 4200 West Salt Lake City, UT 84111 (801) 555-9853

CAREER OBJECTIVE
Seeking a position with a progressive organization, utilizing education and experience in a challenging marketing or sales-related capacity.

EDUCATION
June 1989, Utah State University at Logan, Utah
Bachelor of Science of Marketing

June 1982, Dixie College at St. George, Utah
Associate of Applied Science in Business

June 1980, Lehi High School at Lehi, Utah
Diploma

EXPERIENCE

1987–1989   Nelson's Fine Furnishings, Orem, Utah

Sales Associate
Assisted clients in the selection and purchase of home furnishings, carpet, and related accessories.
Coordinated delivery of products following sale. Also interfaced with representatives of finance and banking organizations in development of financing options.

Accomplishment: Designated as top sales associate for the months of December and January.

1986–1987   Academy Honda, Orem, Utah

Manager (Used Car Division)
Supervised and coordinated sales efforts of four sales representatives in promotion of used automobiles. Provided sales and product information training to new sales associates. Inspected incoming automobiles to determine resale value and negotiated close of sales. Promoted internally from previous position as sales representative.

Accomplishment: Consistently maintained status as top sales representative during tenure.

1985–1986   Camco Construction Company, Salt Lake City, Utah

Carpenter (Commercial Projects)

HONORS AND ACTIVITIES
* Member Utah State University American Marketing Association Chapter
* Dixie College Delta Pi Epsilon Chapter

REFERENCES   Available upon request.

This format is appropriate when your most recent work experience and your educational background relate directly to your future career direction and career goal.

The chronological résumé format is the most traditional of formats. It is easy for employers to read and follow and is generally less difficult than others to prepare. It allows you to emphasize continuity and career growth and will also permit you to stress your most recent employment experience. One of the major disadvantages of the chronological format is that it makes it difficult for you to communicate your general strengths and qualities. Another is that it readily shows gaps of experience and its effectiveness is largely dependent on your previous experiences.

The **functional résumé** format shown in Figure 6.2 permits you to group your experiences under various categories. For example, any of the following categories might be appropriate for broadcasting your strengths to potential employers:

- Work motivation
- Communication
- Problem solving
- Writing skills
- Supervisory skills
- Organizational skills
- Public relations
- Community services
- Voluntary services
- Administrative skills
- Research activities
- Creative talents

After you have identified the categories that represent your strengths, the next step is to include under each of the categories any experience you have gained at any time or place. One of the advantages of the functional format is that it helps you to organize your résumé according to your interests, rather than your past work experience. It will also be helpful if you have not had much prior work experience or if your work experience has been irregular. The major disadvantage of this format is that it downplays any work experience you may have had with a specific employer. The functional format is also sometimes confusing to employers because it is less familiar to them than the chronological format.

The bottom line when choosing a format, however, is that a short, well-organized, and physically attractive résumé will generally be the most effective in communicating your message.

CHRONOLOGICAL RÉSUMÉ

The chronological résumé is the most commonly used format and is widely understood and accepted by employers. Later in this activity, you will prepare a résumé using this format. The following six sections are customarily included when you follow a chronological résumé format:

1. Heading and personal information: name, address, and telephone number (home as well as campus information).
2. Career objectives: the position you are seeking.
3. Education and training: schools/colleges attended, degrees received, dates of completion, major, minor, grade point average, courses of particular interest (relevant courses), and special training received.
4. Honors and activities: awards received, scholarships received, student organizations (offices held), campus activities, professional societies, sports, and other college activities.
5. Experience: work experience, military experience, volunteer positions, special college projects, and hobbies.
6. References: previous employers, teachers, advisors of organizations, and others who will agree to provide you with a character and professional reference in case a potential employer requests them. Instead of actually listing their references, some job applicants prefer to include the statement "Available on request" on their résumés.

Figure 6.2 Functional Résumé

REBECCA THOMPSON	CAMPUS ADDRESS (until 6/1/––) 540 East 300 North #10 Logan, Utah 84321 (801) 555-7564	HOME ADDRESS 3092 North 400 East Ogden, Utah 84402 (801) 555-0338

CAREER OBJECTIVE
A position in public relations that will allow me to use my extensive communication and interpersonal skills in planning, organizing, and implementing promotional or advertising campaigns.

EDUCATION
Utah State University at Logan, Utah
Bachelor of Science in Marketing, June 1989
Minor in Advertising Design
3.67 overall GPA, 3.80 in major

COMMUNICATION
* Verbalizing ideas and concepts to managers, fellow employees, and customers
* Listening and recognizing organizational and customer problems
* Making persuasive sales presentations to prospective customers
* Preparing effective written reports, proposals, and other communication

MANAGEMENT
* Working understanding of performance appraisal as management tool
* Previous supervisory responsibility for 20 employees
* Experience in constructing employees' work schedules

ORGANIZATION
* Prepare annual and monthly budget requests
* Prepare work productivity schedules for advertising department
* Ensure that tasks are completed properly and on time
* Practice sound time-management principles

EMPLOYMENT
* Advertising Sales Associate, Cache Dispatch Weekly, 1986 to present. Supervisor: Laine Farr
* Group Sales Representative, Lagoon Corporation, 1985–1986. Supervisor: Gary Poppleton
* Assistant Mall Manager, Layton Hills Mall, 1984. Supervisor: Helen Wallace

REFERENCES
Personal and professional references available upon request.

IMPORTANT TIPS IN RÉSUMÉ PREPARATION

There are a number of suggestions for developing a winning résumé. Review these tips carefully, and use them when preparing your résumé.

1. Prepare your résumé yourself; you know your own background better than others. Make several copies of your résumé for your files.
2. Make your résumé graphically pleasing by the liberal use of white space and arrangement of information in an artistic fashion.
3. Limit your résumé to one page if possible. Use two pages only if unavoidable. Make your résumé as concise as possible. Other information can be placed on the organization's application form. One rule of thumb is to keep everything short, with no paragraph exceeding ten lines, using phrases where appropriate.
4. Eliminate the use of unnecessary words. Avoid the use of "I," "he," and "she" as you describe your work or educational experience.
5. Use action verbs such as "supervised," "constructed," "managed," "developed," "prepared," "planned," etc., in describing your work or educational experience.
6. Spend some extra time preparing your statement of career objective so that it matches as closely as possible the position(s) that might be available. Your career objective should be placed immediately after the personal information section of your résumé. In your cover letter, include a direct reference to your career objective.
7. Prepare your résumé to show what you can do for the employer and what value you will have to the organization.
8. If your résumé includes personal and professional references, be sure to ask these people for permission in advance. Provide adequate information on how to reach these individuals.
9. Before you submit your résumé in final form for printing or photocopying, proofread all the information very carefully. Typographical and spelling errors are inexcusable. Consider having a friend with good English skills or a faculty member proofread your résumé before it is reproduced.
10. Prepare the final draft of your résumé in a professional manner. Use of a microcomputer and a laser printer (or other letter-quality printer) will enhance the appearance of your résumé. Consider using a professional printer or résumé service for the final preparation of your résumé.

Prior to actually preparing your résumé, there are several concepts you should have clearly in mind. On the basis of the information provided in this text, as well as your own experience, answer the following questions.

1. What are the four major purposes of completing a résumé?

   a.

   b.

   c.

   d.

2. How will a résumé help you gain confidence in yourself?

3. How will a well-prepared résumé help you obtain a job interview?

4. Which of the two formats for résumé preparation will you select, and why?

Format _____

What is your reason for choosing this format?

5. What are the six major sections commonly included in a chronological résumé?

a.

b.

c.

d.

e.

f.

COMPLETING THE SIX SECTIONS OF A RÉSUMÉ

The easiest way to start your résumé is to prepare each section separately before putting them all together. As each section is explained below, please complete all the information requested. Then combine them into a complete draft of your résumé.

Heading and Personal Information

Include your name, address (college and permanent), and telephone numbers where you can be reached. Your name may be used in the heading for your résumé.

Résumé of (your name) _____

Campus Address	**Home Address**
Street _____	_____
City and state _____	_____
Zip code _____	_____
Telephone (AC) _____	_____

Career Objective

The statement of your career objective should be a strong, concise, simple sentence stating exactly the type of job or position you are seeking. Your career objective should be written to convince a potential employer that you are the right match for the position(s) available in that organization. Your career objective should describe the skills, abilities, and qualities you are offering the organization. It is important to understand that, whenever possible, the career objective section of your résumé should be customized to the position for which you are applying. **If you cannot write a good, clear career objective, omit this section on your résumé.** An example of a poorly written career objective might read as follows:

> "To obtain a challenging position of responsibility, offering me training and advancement with a goal-oriented organization."

A better way of writing this objective would be:

"To obtain a challenging position in personnel administration requiring effective communication, human relations, problem-solving, and organizational skills."

Please complete the following related to your career objective:

Title of position sought _____

Statement of your career objective _____

_____

_____

_____

Education and Training

Identify schools attended, date(s) completed, major, minor, grade point average, courses of particular interest, and training received. List your education and training background in reverse chronological order; that is, your most recent education and training should be listed first (end with your high school). Please complete the following:

College(s) attended _____

Date of graduation or expected date of graduation _____

College major _____ GPA _____

College minor _____ GPA _____

Courses taken related to career objective

_____

_____

_____

High school attended _____

Date of graduation _____

Major course of study _____

Grade point average or rank in class _____

Specific skills mastered as a result of education

_____

_____

_____

Specialized training completed

_____

_____

_____

Specific skills mastered as a result of training

_____

_____

_____

Honors and Activities

Identify honors received and activities in which you have engaged while in school and college. The purpose of this section is to show employers that you have taken part in activities other than school and work, that you have a range of interests and abilities, and that you have something special to offer. How far back you go in this section depends partly on the number of honors received and variety of activities you have been involved with since leaving high school. If the list is long, you will probably choose not to include high school activities. Otherwise you may want to broaden the list by mentioning some earlier experiences. Items that can be included in this section may vary but generally include scholarships received, awards received, student organization participation and offices held, professional societies, and sports. In the space provided, please list any honors you received and activities you participated in while in school.

Honors _____

_____

Activities _____

_____

_____

Experience

Include work experience, military experience, volunteer positions held, special college projects, and hobbies. List your most recent work experience first. Following each position, you should include a short statement about your job responsibilities, special job projects, job accomplishments, number of people supervised, recognitions, and so forth. Use action verbs to describe these responsibilities. For example, rather than just saying that you were employed as an engineering draftsperson, say something like this: "Engineering draftsperson. Completed drafting layout work for $50,000 project." Please complete the following as it relates to your own work experience.

Most Recent Employer

Job Title _____ Dates employed _____

Name and address of employing organization _____

_____

Name of immediate supervisor_____

Statement of duties and responsibilities _____

_____

Second Most Recent Employer

Job title _____ Dates employed _____

Name and address of employing organization _____

_____

Name of immediate supervisor _____

Statement of duties and responsibilities _____

_____

Next Most Recent Employer

Job title _____ Dates employed _____

Name and address of employing organization _____

_____

Name of immediate supervisor _____

Statement of duties and responsibilities _____

_____

Other experiences:

_____

_____

References

Include the names, addresses, and telephone numbers of individuals who you believe would provide you with a positive recommendation should they be contacted by a prospective employer. People you might consider naming as references are those who know of your abilities and skills, your attitude, your working habits, and your character. College teachers in your major field of study, previous job supervisors, and significant members of your community should be considered. If you list references, make sure that you have received prior permission from each person. If you do not give names, whether for space or other reasons, it is considered acceptable to say "References available upon request." In the space provided, list the names, titles, organizations, and phone numbers of three potential references:

Name _____

Title _____

Organization _____

Address _____

Telephone _____

Name _____

Title _____

Organization _____

Address _____

Telephone _____

Name _____

Title _____

Organization _____

Address _____

Telephone _____

COMPLETING YOUR RÉSUMÉ

You have now prepared all the information needed for your complete résumé. The next step is to identify the section titles you will use and transfer the information you have already recorded to a rough draft of your résumé. This activity has recommended titles for six sections of a résumé. You may use these section titles or substitute others that better advertise your talents and strengths. In the space provided, choose exact section titles and put them in the order that best suits you. You may choose to omit a particular section title if you believe that your background is inadequate or lacking in that area.

Section Titles for Your Résumé

Section 1 (Compulsory): Personal Information (title may be omitted)

Section 2 _____

Section 3 _____

Section 4 _____

Section 5 _____

Section 6 _____

Now you are ready to transfer the information you have recorded earlier in this activity to a rough draft of your résumé. Use several sheets of blank paper to prepare this draft. Refer back to Figures 6.1 and 6.2 for layout ideas. When you have completed the draft, ask a friend, a faculty member, or someone from your college's placement office to critique it. Taking suggestions into consideration, prepare a final copy of your résumé. Insist on a professional appearance. The American Marketing Association, in its *Employment Kit*[1] for college students, recommends the following tips regarding the actual physical preparation of a résumé:

1. Use a clear carbon-based typewriter ribbon or, if using a microcomputer, be sure to utilize a letter-quality printer.
2. Use one-inch margins on all sides.
3. Don't make it look cramped.
4. Highlight using caps, underlining, italics, or bold print.
5. Use single space, but double between paragraphs and triple between sections.
6. Select the highest quality paper (20 to 26 lb.), preferably in white or off-white.
7. Use typeset printing or clean photocopying.
8. If you use two pages, number the second and include your name. No address is needed.

Figures 6.3 and 6.4 also offer suggestions you would be wise to bear in mind.

PREPARING AN APPLICATION LETTER

A résumé such as the one you developed in this activity should never be sent to an employer without a typed cover letter. This letter, referred to as a **letter of application,** should be tailored as much as possible to the target organization. Make every effort to address a letter of application to a specific individual within the organization. You can usually determine the proper name by telephoning the central office of the organization.

Application letters should be brief, businesslike, and to the point. Three or four paragraphs should be adequate to cover all necessary content.

Paragraph 1.   State your purpose in writing. Identify the type of job, or the actual job, for which you are applying. If you saw the position announcement posted in the co-op/ internship or placement office, name the specific position and mention where you saw the notice.

Paragraph 2.   Identify your career objective and highlight your qualifications that are relevant to the position. You may also state why you believe you would be the best possible candidate for the job.

Paragraph 3.   State that you are enclosing a current résumé and ask for information on what steps you should take next. Or request a personal interview, indicating that you will call to arrange a suitable time.

---

[1] American Marketing Association, *The Employment Kit: A Practical Guide to Achieving Success in the Job Market* (American Marketing Association, 250 So. Wacker Dr., Chicago, IL 60606-5819), 1986.

REVIEWING MATERIALS AVAILABLE ON
YOUR CAMPUS

Most colleges that have ongoing cooperative education/internship programs provide handbooks and other materials that describe their program. Obtain copies of these publications and, in the space provided, list their titles. Reading these promotional materials will give you a better understanding of your college's cooperative/internship program.

Figure 6.3

Do's and Don'ts

DO

- Take your time. In the drafting stage, write everything that demonstrates skill—babysitting, handiwork, counseling fellow students.
- Check for spelling and grammar.
- Translate duties to skills, accomplishments, responsibilities.
- Leave out the word "I" and get right to the point; "Coached cheerleaders in team coordination for two seasons."

DON'T

- Think you can write it perfectly in one half-hour sitting.
- Be overly critical of yourself in writing the first draft. Save the criticism for the editing stage.
- Write in a language (vernacular) known mostly on your campus, but not easily understood by others.
- Describe duties or ever use that word.
- Take too long to say too little: "I pulled together seven cheerleaders and helped them be sensitive to working as a team in order to . . ."

SOURCE: College Placement Council, *CPC Annual,* 30th Ed., Vol. 1, 1986–87, p. 21. Reprinted with the permission of the College Placement Council and Thomas W. Jackson.

Figure 6.4

RÉSUMÉS: HOW WELL PRINTED	*APPEARANCE COUNTS.* In the spring, a college senior's fancy turns to graduation, jobs—and résumés. When preparing those résumés, pay attention to the quality of the printing, advises the "Journal of Business Communications." It found that poor printing can do almost as much damage to job prospects as poor grades. In a study, 32 executives rated résumés from five accounting graduates seeking an entry-level position. The bosses gave top marks to a professionally printed résumé on heavy white paper, followed by a typeset résumé on colored paper, a high-quality photocopy, a smudged and lined photocopy and a photocopied résumé with decidedly inferior qualifications.

SOURCE: Copyright, 1987, *U.S. News and World Report.* Reprinted from issue of March 9, 1987.

Paragraph 4.   Thank the reader for his or her consideration. You may provide a telephone number where you can be reached or where a message can be left. You might also specify the date when you will be available for work.

There is no one formula for writing an effective application letter, so use the suggestions for these paragraphs as guidelines only. Many of the items may shift to other paragraphs in order to strengthen your letter and make it more effective. Be sure that your final letter is neatly typed, and check thoroughly for any spelling or grammatical errors.

Examine the sample letter of application shown in Figure 6.5. Then prepare a letter of application that you could send with your résumé to a prospective employer.

Figure 6.5   Sample Cover Letter for Résumé

```
                                        Your street address
                                        City, State ZIP code
                                        Current date


        Inside address
        (Direct to an individual if possible)

        Dear ——:

        This April I will be eligible for a cooperative
        education/internship assignment in my major field, which
        is data processing technology. I am interested in
        completing my cooperative education/internship experience
        as a computer programmer in your organization's data
        processing department.

        An announcement posted in our college's cooperative
        education/internship office states that your organization
        has a position opening for a programmer. As a data
        processing major at City Community College, I believe that
        my training background and career objective would be of
        interest to your organization. I have completed 12
        semester credit hours in the data processing field,
        including introduction to data processing, data processing
        operations, BASIC programming, and COBOL Programming.
        Currently I am also serving as the secretary for the CCC
        chapter of Data Processing Managers Association (DPMA).

        Enclosed is a copy of my current resume. I would be happy
        to complete an application form for employment with your
        organization and to make myself available for a personal
        interview at your convenience. I will call your office
        next week to determine what steps I should follow in
        completing the application process.

        Thank you for your assistance in this important matter.
        Your review of my resume and favorable consideration for
        an interview would be appreciated.

                                        Sincerely,

                                        (your signature)

                                        Typed name

        Enclosure
```

ACTIVITY 7
Completing Application Forms and Letters

Purpose: To provide you with information necessary to complete an application form successfully, as required for employment in a cooperative education/internship position. To expose you to examples of typical letters used in the employment process.

At some point in the preemployment process you will be required to complete an application form. If you are interviewed on campus for a cooperative education/internship position, you will usually be expected to fill out an application prior to the interview. Occasionally, however, you will be asked to do so following an on-campus interview or, if you make a trip to the organization's central office, prior to that visit. If you contact potential employers directly, you will nearly always be required to complete the form prior to being granted an interview.

A résumé like the one you prepared in Activity 6 is usually not accepted as a substitute for a completed application form. A résumé is designed to present you in the most favorable light, whereas application forms may ask for information that you have purposely omitted. Employers use forms to make sure that the information they collect is uniform among applicants. Most application forms also contain a place for your signature, which is your verification that the information presented is accurate and complete.

Although it may sound unlikely to you as a college student, many people fail to get the job they want because they have trouble filling out the form. The application form is an important selection tool for employers in the hiring process. It serves as a screening device—a way of eliminating undesirable or unqualified applicants. A neatly and accurately completed application form is a prerequisite to getting the job interview. It is also the employer's first look at you as a prospective employee and thus should present a positive first impression.

Much of the information required on a company's application form can be taken from the résumé you drafted in Activity 6. Sometimes you will be able to complete an application form away from the employer's office. You should, however, be prepared to complete the form on the employer's premises.

The application form is used at all points in the hiring process. It is the applicant's main method (and often the only method) of showing his or her good points to an employer. In many organizations, someone in the personnel office makes judgments about an applicant on the basis of the application form, without ever seeing the person. The applicant's answers on the form are often used to decide whether the applicant is qualified for the job opening and should be considered for the job. In many cases applicants receive ratings or scores solely on the basis of the information provided on the application.

PARTS OF A TYPICAL JOB APPLICATION FORM

Most job applications request similar types of information. Of course, some forms are more comprehensive than others, requiring more detailed and specific job-related information. Generally speaking, the information requested on application forms can be divided into seven major parts.

1. Identification information (personal information)
   a. Name
   b. Current address and telephone number
   c. Permanent address and telephone number
   d. Social security number
   e. Date of application
2. Educational and training background
   a. High school attended (date completed, grade point average, ranking, etc.)
   b. College(s) attended (dates of attendance, grade point average, major and minor fields of study, class ranking, GPA, etc.)
   c. Honors and activities
   d. Special training received
   e. Certificates and licenses
3. Position desired
   a. Position title applied for
   b. Date available to start
   c. Salary expected
4. Experience
   a. Previous employment experience
   b. Description of positions and duties
   c. Reason for leaving previous positions
   d. Time periods of employment
   e. Salary history
   f. Military experience (may be included as part of employment history)
5. Extracurricular activities
   a. Volunteer activities
   b. Professional organization memberships
   c. Clubs and organizations
   d. Hobbies and other interests
   e. Leisure-time activities
6. References
   a. Names and addresses of references
   b. Telephone numbers of references
   c. Number of years references have known you
   d. Relationship of references to you
   e. Permission to contact references
7. Miscellaneous information
   a. Security clearances
   b. Future goals and plans

Carefully examine the application form in Figure 7.1. In the space provided here, identify questions or sections that you do not understand. Discuss any confusing or unclear items with a cooperative education/internship coordinator or someone in the placement office.

Confusing or Unclear Items	Explanation
1.	
2.	
3.	
4.	
5.	

Figure 7.1 Application for Employment

Date of Application _____

We consider applicants for all positions without regard to race, color, religion, sex, national origin, age, marital or veteran status, the presence of a non-job-related medical condition or handicap, or any other legally protected status.

General Information

Name			Date	Work Desired
Street Address			Phone Number	Full-time _____ Part-time _____ Seasonal _____ Temporary _____
City	State	ZIP	Social Security Number	

Have you filed an application here before?   ☐ Yes ☐ No   If yes, give date _____

Have you ever been employed here before? ☐ Yes ☐ No   If yes, give date _____

Are you employed now? ☐ Yes ☐ No   May we contact your present employer? ☐ Yes ☐ No

Position(s) Applied For _____ Date You Can Start _____ Salary Desired _____

If related to anyone in our employ, state name and position _____

Education

	Elementary					High				College/ University				Graduate/ Professional			
School Name																	
Years Completed/Degree	4	5	6	7	8	9	10	11	12	1	2	3	4	1	2	3	4
Diploma/Degree																	
Describe Course Of Study:																	

Honors Received

_____

_____

_____

Specialized Training, Apprenticeship, Special Skills, and Extra-Curricular Activities

_____

_____

_____

Figure 7.1 Application for Employment (continued)

Employment Experience

Start with your present or last job. Include military service assignments and volunteer activities. You may exclude organization names which indicate race, color, religion, gender, national origin, handicap or other protected status.

Employer	Telephone ( )	Dates Employed		Work Performed
		From	To	
Address				
Job Title		Hourly Rate/Salary		
		Starting	Final	
Supervisor				
Reason for Leaving				
Employer	Telephone ( )	Dates Employed		Work Performed
		From	To	
Address				
Job Title		Hourly Rate/Salary		
		Starting	Final	
Supervisor				
Reason for Leaving				
Employer	Telephone ( )	Dates Employed		Work Performed
		From	To	
Address				
Job Title		Hourly Rate/Salary		
		Starting	Final	
Supervisor				
Reason for Leaving				

If you need additional space, please continue on a separate sheet of paper.

Do you have any physical handicap which you feel would prevent you from performing certain kinds of work without significantly increasing the hazards to yourself, to others, or the work facility, or which would prevent substantial work performance? ☐ Yes ☐ No

If yes, describe work limitations. _____

Have you been convicted of a felony within the last 7 years? ☐ No ☐ Yes
(Conviction will not necessarily disqualify applicant from employment.)

If yes, please explain. _____

Are you prevented from lawfully becoming employed in this country because of Visa or Immigrant Status? ☐ No ☐ Yes (Proof of citizenship or immigration status will be required upon employment.)

I certify that answers given herein are true and complete to the best of my knowledge.

In the event of employment, I understand that false or misleading information given in my application or interview(s) may result in discharge. I understand, also, that I am required to abide by all rules and regulations of the employer.

_____   _____
Signature of Applicant   Date

Completing Application Forms and Letters

FILLING OUT AN APPLICATION FORM COMPLETELY AND ACCURATELY

A neat and accurately completed job application form is often your first step toward securing employment. Here are a number of tips or suggestions you should keep in mind when you fill out an application:

1. Before you begin filling out the form, read all sections thoroughly. Follow all specific directions. Many applications begin by stating that the application form should be printed in ink or typewritten.

2. Be sure to have your résumé on hand for ready reference as you fill out the application. Avoid referring employers to information contained on your attached résumé.

3. If you complete the form at the employer's office, be sure you have brought along the proper tools. These should include an erasable black pen, a small dictionary, your résumé (to leave with employer), and a list of references with addresses and phone numbers.

4. You should answer all questions except those that do not legally require an answer. Questions relating to sex, age, religion, marital status, and race are illegal, and you are not required to answer them. If there are questions on the application form that do not apply to you, use a short dash (—) or write "NA" ("not applicable") after the question. This tells the employer that you have read the question and that it does not apply to you. If, however, the question does apply to you and the answer you would provide might lead to a negative impression or a misunderstanding, you can choose to leave that line blank on the application. Or you can write in the blank: "Will discuss during interview."

5. The spaces provided on application forms for answers are usually quite limited. Be careful to use the correct line for your response and select the wording that will most nearly meet the employer's expectations. Correct spelling, short but descriptive responses, and readability are very important.

6. If possible, obtain two copies of the application form. Print the first copy in pencil as neatly as you can. Have another qualified person review your penciled copy before you prepare your final copy.

7. The work history or experience portion of the application is probably the most important part. In your work history, account in a positive way for any significant periods of time when you were not working. Be sure to provide complete information, including addresses, phone numbers, and names of your previous supervisors if requested. Again, don't substitute a résumé for this section.

8. Make sure your finished application form gets to the right place at the right time. Frequently employers set deadlines or closing dates, after which they won't accept your application. Applications received after the deadline or closing date are often disregarded.

9. When you claim college studies related to the qualifications for the position, submit complete transcripts showing the course work you have completed. Do not send letters of recommendation or copies of any awards you may have received.

10. Always provide a telephone number where you can be reached. Employers like to make interview appointments by telephone. Usually they don't want to write a letter and then wait for a reply from you. If you don't have a phone number where you can be reached easily, find a neighbor, friend, or relative who can take a message for you.

COMPLETING YOUR APPLICATION

Figure 7.1 is a fairly typical application form, but you should compare the variety of application forms used by different companies. Obtain application forms from several companies, and practice using the suggestions given above as you complete one of the forms. Then ask a professional staff member from the cooperative education/internship office or placement office to review it. On a separate sheet of paper, summarize this person's critique.

SAMPLE LETTERS

In Activity 6 you prepared a letter of application that could be sent with your résumé to a prospective employer. If you are mailing an application to an employer, a cover letter should always accompany it. An example of a cover letter for an application is shown in Figure 7.2. In the process of seeking employment you will also need to prepare thank-you letters, letters of acceptance, and letters of refusal. Study the samples of each of these letters, which are shown in Figures 7.3, 7.4, and 7.5.

Figure 7.2   Sample Cover Letter for Application

(Sent with a completed application form to the prospective employer.)

```
                                    Your street address
                                    City, State ZIP code
                                    Current date


        Address to an individual if possible
        Company name
        Street address
        City, State ZIP code

        Dear (use correct form of address—Miss, Ms., Mrs., Mr.,
        Sir, or Madam)

        Enclosed you will find my completed application for the
        position of (name of position) with (name of
        organization). This position was (identify where the
        position was posted or advertised or who told you about
        the position).

        (Identify your career objective, highlight your
        qualifications that are relevant to the position, and
        state why you believe you would be the best candidate
        for the job.)

        I would like to arrange for a personal interview at your
        convenience. I can be reached at home at (714) 555-3189,
        or a message may be left at (714) 555-2173.

        Thank you for your consideration. Your review of my
        application and favorable consideration for an interview
        would be appreciated.

                                    Sincerely,

                                    (your signature)

                                    Typed name


        Enclosure
```

Figure 7.3   Sample Thank-You Letter

(Sent to the individual who interviewed you for a cooperative education/internship position.)

```
                                        Your address
                                        City, State ZIP code
                                        Current date


        Inside address
        (Direct to an individual if possible)

        Dear ——:

        Thank you for meeting with me on (date) regarding
        prospective employment as (title of position) with
        (name of organization). The information and ideas you
        presented to me during the interview were interesting
        and thought provoking. I am excited about the
        possibility of completing my cooperative education/
        internship assignment with an outstanding
        organization such as yours, which will allow me to
        make use of my experience and education.

        If you need any additional information, please do not
        hesitate to contact me. I look forward to hearing
        from you in the near future.

                                        Sincerely,

                                        (your signature)

                                        Typed name
```

Figure 7.4   Sample Letter of Acceptance

(Sent to an employer who has offered employment.)

```
                                        Your address
                                        City, State ZIP code
                                        Current date


            Inside address
            (Direct to an individual if possible)

            Dear ——:

            Thank you for offering me employment as a (name
            of position) with (name of organization). My
            understanding of the offer is that (details of offer:
            starting date, location, salary, etc.). I am pleased
            to accept your offer and look forward to meeting with
            you at (time, day, date).

            (Identify any enclosure included such as papers
            required by the personnel office.)

            I am looking forward to a valuable experience during
            my co-op/internship assignment with your
            organization. I am confident that I can meet or
            exceed your expectations.

                                        Sincerely,

                                        (your signature)

                                        Typed name
```

Figure 7.5   Sample Letter of Refusal

(Sent to an employer who makes you an employment offer that you have decided not to accept.)

```
                                        Your address
                                        City, State ZIP code
                                        Current date


            Inside address
            (Direct to an individual if possible)

            Dear ——:

            Thank you for offering me a position as a (title
            of position) with (name of organization). I am
            honored to have been selected for the position;
            however, I am unable to accept your offer at this
            time. This is a difficult decision, but I have
            decided to accept a position with another
            organization.

            Thank you very much for your time and consideration.
            I sincerely appreciate all your efforts on my behalf,
            as well as the confidence you have shown in me.

                                  Sincerely,

                                  (your signature)

                                  Typed name
```

Name _____   Date _____

ACTIVITY 8
Understanding Testing and Its Legal Implications

Purpose: To present information regarding preemployment screening and to discuss the legal implications of testing and other issues related to employment.

"With very few exceptions, cooperative education student placements are considered common law employment, altered only by a particular arrangement whereby the cooperative education assignment is an integral part of the student's baccalaureate degree program at an institution of higher education. Therefore, a cooperative education student is subject to laws, rights, and limitations that apply to the employer–employee relationship."[1] The case of unpaid interns is not as clear. In a Department of Labor publication, trainees are distinguished from employees as follows: "Whether trainees or students are employees of an employer under the Act [Fair Labor Standards Act] will depend upon all of the circumstances surrounding their activities on the premises of the employer."[2] The pamphlet then lists six criteria that must apply. It is criterion number four that contains the problem in interpretation, when it states: "The employer that provides the training derives no immediate advantage from the activities of the trainees or students."[3] Therefore, if an employer derives benefit from the services of the worker, then the worker *must* be paid.

Yet some types of internships are excluded from this requirement when the training is essential for licensing regulations. Therefore, student teaching and clinical practice for nurses, therapists, laboratory technicians, medical interns, and so forth are excluded. Suffice it to say that in your co-op/internship program you are probably considered an employee rather than a student. This provision also means that any wages earned are subject to income tax.

PRESCREENING OF APPLICANTS

In 1978, the Equal Employment Opportunity Commission, the Departments of Justice and Labor, and the U.S. Civil Service Commission developed their *Uniform Guidelines on Employee Selection Procedures*. The guidelines prohibit anyone from making employment decisions using selection criteria that might have an adverse impact on the employment opportunities for minorities, women, and other groups. Protected groups now include older workers and qualified handicapped individuals as well. In some states the guidelines have been interpreted to include the sexual orientation of applicants. Selection procedures are defined as "Any measure, combination of measures, or procedure used as a basis for any employment decision. Selection procedures include the full range of assessment techniques from traditional paper and pencil tests, performance

---

[1] Department of Cooperative Education, *Employee Cooperative Education Students* (Boston: Northeastern University, n.d.): 1.

[2] U.S. Department of Labor, Employment Relationships under the Fair Labor Standards Act (Washington, D.C.: U.S. Government Printing Office, February 1973): 7.

[3] Ibid., pp. 7 and 8.

tests, training programs or probationary periods, and physical, educational and work experience requirements through information or casual interviews and unscored application forms.''[4]

To establish compliance, employers may have to demonstrate that their criteria (1) do not have an adverse impact on any specific group and (2) are necessary to performance in the position. It is in this context that questions arise regarding preemployment drug testing. This issue had not received attention from the courts or legislative bodies as of the printing of this book. A 1987 decision by the Ninth Circuit U.S. Court of Appeals affirmed that AIDS could not be used as grounds for denying employment if a person is otherwise qualified to perform his or her job.[5]

However, inquiries regarding age, sex, ethnic or religious background, marital status, and the like have been on the list of prohibited questions for prospective employees for more than a decade. What does this mean to you, as an applicant for a cooperative education/internship position? It means substantially the same to you as to any other prospective employee. The criteria used for selection must be related to the job requirements and cannot be discriminatory on the basis of age, sex, ethnic or religious group, handicapping condition (if otherwise qualified), and, in some states, sexual orientation.

In the following list of personal characteristics, place an "X" beside the items you think employers would be prohibited from asking.

_____ 1. Grade point average

_____ 2. Sex (male or female)

_____ 3. Major in college

_____ 4. Home town

_____ 5. Place of birth

_____ 6. Date of birth

_____ 7. Past criminal record

_____ 8. Year of graduation from high school

_____ 9. Date of expected graduation from college

_____ 10. Married or single

_____ 11. Birthplace of parents

_____ 12. Past medical history

_____ 13. Religion

_____ 14. Your age

If you marked 2, 4, 5, 6, 7, 10, 11, 12, 13, and 14, you were correct. These questions are prohibited during the employment selection process. Numbers 1 and 3 may be prohibited if the employer cannot justify the need or if they are shown to discriminate against certain groups. Number 8 can be a means of ascertaining age and therefore may not be allowed. If you have questions regarding any of your answers, please ask your cooperative education/internship coordinator.

More and more employers are requiring preemployment drug screening, although the issue has not yet been tested in the courts. As a prospective employee, you may be required to submit to such testing if you wish to be hired. Employers, both public and private, use testing to detect evidence of drugs and alcohol. Yet there remain many questions as to the accuracy, reliability, and

---

[4] Equal Employment Opportunity Commission, U.S. Department of Justice, U.S. Department of Labor, and U.S. Civil Service Commission, *Uniform Guidelines on Employee Selection Procedures* (Washington, D.C.: U.S. Government Printing Office, 1978): Sec. 10.

[5] College Placement Council, *CPC Spotlight* (Jan. 4, 1988): 2.

legality of such tests. The sample letter in Figure 8.1 is typical of those received routinely by college placement officers from the firms that recruit on campus.

LEGAL IMPLICATIONS FOR CO-OPS AND INTERNS

In addition to the legal and ethical issues that you might face during the selection process, there are other requirements that may affect you once you have been hired.

Income Taxes

In general, all payments received by cooperative education/internship students are considered wages and thus subject to provisions of the Internal Revenue Code. This means that taxes will be withheld and that you must complete an IRS W-4 form. Likewise, you must report these earnings on your annual income tax report.

Minimum Wages, Hours, and Overtime Pay

Cooperative education/internship students are included under the Fair Labor Standards Act, except in certain positions that may be exempt by the special nature of the position. This means that employers must observe the provisions for minimum wages, hours, and overtime pay. Check with your program coordinator if you have questions in this regard.

Employment of Foreign Students

If U.S. citizenship or a security clearance is not required as a condition of employment, employers may hire foreign students with F-1 visas who are referred by the cooperative education department. If no compensation is provided (as is the case with many internship programs), then students with F-1 visas are also eligible to participate. When compensation is involved, even if it is in the form of room and board, foreign students *may* receive such compensation if they are "enrolled in a college, university, or seminary having alternate work-study courses as part of its regular prescribed curriculum."[6] However, permission must be granted in each case by the U.S. Immigration and Naturalization Service.

Unemployment Compensation

The Federal Unemployment Tax Act of 1970 (FUTA) and its amendments lists under "Exclusions for Employment" an "individual under the age of 22 who is enrolled at a non-profit or public educational institution . . . which combines academic instruction with work experience, if the service is an integral part of the program." However, the program is administered by each state and the provisions vary depending upon appropriate state statutes.

In some states, cooperative education students of any age are excluded. In those states, students who may be laid off from their assignments are not eligible to collect unemployment compensation, and it is illegal for them to do so. Likewise, employers of those students do not have to pay federal or state unemployment tax on the cooperative students' wages. In other states where the laws differ, cooperative students over the age of 22 may be eligible to collect benefits and the employers may have to pay taxes on their wages. Your cooperative education/internship coordinator should be able to tell you what the law is in your state.

Worker's Compensation

In most states, cooperative education students are covered by the Worker's Compensation Act under the employer's insurance. If paid employment is not involved, the issue is considerably

---

[6] U.S. Immigration and Naturalization Service, Immigration Service Form I-538, Paragraph C, "Practical Training."

Figure 8.1 Sample Letter Announcing Drug Testing

Fairfield Corporation
FC 10 Meadowlake Drive
Sunnyvale, CA 94087-2018

June 15, 19—

To: Placement Directors

This is to advise you that, effective immediately,
our company will require drug testing as part of its
preemployment process for all applicants. Employment
offers extended to potential new hires, including
cooperative education students, will be conditional
upon their passing a preemployment physical
examination, which includes a drug test to determine
the presence of illegal or unauthorized drugs in
their system.

Since we actively recruit at your institution, we
would appreciate your informing all students
interested in seeking permanent, cooperative, and
summer employment of this company policy.

Thank you for your cooperation.

                            R. A. Gamble
                            Director, Corporate Personnel

mh

more cloudy. It is possible that, in the case of injury on the job, the responsibility for providing coverage may be shifted to the educational institution. In either case, you as the student employee are covered in the event of accident or injury on the job. You should find out what the laws are in the state in which you are employed by contacting the appropriate agency in that state. Once again, check with your coordinator.

Clinical Malpractice

If you are employed in a position where there is the danger of injury to patients through clinical malpractice, it is possible that the same malpractice insurance that covers you during your academic clinical experiences will also cover you during the cooperative education/internship experience. This is true only if your college has made that arrangement with the insurance carrier. Again, check with your coordinator or counselor.

Privacy of Records

Under the Family Rights and Privacy Act, your records are confidential and cannot be shared with a prospective employer without your permission. Confidential information includes your grades and your GPA. Any portfolio, dossier, or other file containing references, résumés, and so forth can be forwarded only with your permission. You, however, have the right, under the regulations set forth by your educational institution, to see your own institutional records. This right extends to any files, whatever their form, including unofficial records and informal notes. What do you wish to have shared with a prospective employer? Make a list of the items you might send or bring with you to enhance your chances for obtaining the job. You also have the right to examine your employer's written evaluation of you, even if the employer does not discuss it with you.

ACTIVITY 9
Preparing for a Successful Job Interview

Purpose: To help you better understand how you can prepare for the job interview process.

The job interview is the most critical step in the total employment process. In most cases it is the job interview that will win or lose you the job. Your goal in the job interview is to market or sell yourself to prospective employers. You are the product; the interviewer and the organization are the consumer. Your goal during the interview is to show how you will meet the needs of the organization. The job interview is not a one-way process, however. Not only is the interviewer trying to determine if you will fulfill the organization's needs but you want to find out if this organization meets your employment needs.

Job interviews can be classified into two categories. The first is the **screening interview,** by which the interviewer reviews a large number of applicants. The major purpose of this type of interview is to eliminate all but a few applicants. The résumé becomes the interviewer's primary basis for questions. The interviewer will look for weaknesses, gaps, and inconsistencies in the résumé. The interviewer is also trying to determine if your résumé is a true reflection of you and, if so, whether your qualifications meet the requirements of the available position. Figure 9.1 is an example of a typical screening interview evaluation form.

The second type of interview, the **selection interview,** is likely to be conducted by the person to whom you will report if you get the job. This person is probably not trained as an interviewer and is more interested in how you will fit into the organization than in your professional credentials.

PREPARING IN ADVANCE FOR A JOB INTERVIEW

Time spent in preparation for the interview will give you a head start in the job interview process. To sell or market yourself effectively, you first need to understand that interviewers are seeking the best qualified applicant for the position. Here are items sometimes used to determine the qualifications of an applicant:

1. Education and training relevant to the available position
2. Previous work experience that relates to the position
3. Skills that are applicable to the position (a person who can operate a microcomputer can easily learn how to use a software package used by the company)
4. Indications of success or ability to achieve results (for example, GPA, leadership positions, teamwork capabilities, membership in organizations, honors)
5. Personal characteristics such as attitude, creativity, ability to communicate, adaptability, determination, charisma, and personality.

Prior to the interview, you can do a number of things to ensure that you are adequately prepared. First, you can learn about the interviewing organization. Second, you can spend some time assessing what you consider to be your own strengths and weaknesses, and you can learn how to prove a strength. Third, you can practice how to respond to typical interview questions and

Figure 9.1   Sample Screening Interview Evaluation

Title of job opening: _____

Name of applicant: _____

Address and phone number: _____

Name of interviewer: _____

Date of interview: _____

Qualifications	Superior	Acceptable	Unacceptable
1. Educational background			
2. Special technical skills			
3. Past work experience background			
4. Attitude			
5. Adaptability (ability to relocate)			
6. Appearance and grooming			
7. Overall personality			
8. Communication skills required for success			
9. Interest and enthusiasm			

Other comments:

Overall evaluation: ___ Reject
                                      ___ Second interview
                                      ___ Offer employment

learn how to handle objections the interviewer might raise. Finally, you can prepare questions to ask the interviewer.

RESEARCHING THE INTERVIEWING ORGANIZATION

Before you interview, you should find out as much as possible about the interviewing organization. In Activity 5 you developed a list of potential employers and the contact person in each organization. Before interviewing with any of these organizations, you must research the organization more thoroughly. Be prepared to answer such questions as "Why are you interested in our organization?" or "Why did you choose to interview with our organization?" College and local public libraries often subscribe to directories such as Dun & Bradstreet's *Million Dollar Directory,* Standard & Poor's *Register of Corporations, Directors & Executives,* and *Standard Directory of Advertisers,* which answer many questions about certain businesses and organizations. Many career placement and cooperative education/internship offices also maintain directories or complete files on selected organizations.

Before your interview, you should be able to answer the following questions about the organization. Use any of the suggested references to help you answer these questions.

1. What is the complete name and address of the organization?

2. Where (in what city and state) is the main office for the organization? Where are its branches or subdivisions?

3. The organization is involved in what type of activity? Is it a manufacturing, service, or nonprofit organization? What is the growth potential for this type of organization?

4. What is the total amount of annual sales or income of the organization? What is the size of the organization relative to others of the same type?

5. What is the total number of employees working in the organization?

6. What other information about the organization do you think would be of value to you during the interview?

7. What types of career opportunities in your field are available in the organization? Does the organization offer a formal training program?

8. How do you think a person with your background can make a contribution to the organization?

ASSESSING YOUR STRENGTHS AND WEAKNESSES

Prior to the interview you need to spend some time assessing what you consider to be your major strengths and weaknesses. For example, a strength might be several years of related part-time work experience while attending school. Another strength might be your leadership ability or your strong communication skills. A weakness, on the other hand, might be that as a result of your tight work/school schedule, your grade point average is only 2.6. Or, perhaps you have been criticized in the past for your short temper. Identify what you consider to be your major strengths and weaknesses. After listing each strength, explain how it has been developed through school work, activities, or work experience. For each weakness, specify what you are doing to improve in that area.

Strengths Assessment

Strengths	How Developed or Proof of Statement
Example: Organizational ability	Served as president of the student organization Phi Beta Lambda.

1.

2.

3.

4.

5.

Weaknesses Assessment

Weaknesses	Possible Remediation, Solution, or Improvement
Example: Tendency to take on more than time will permit me to accomplish	Develop better time management skills, including how to set priorities.

1.

2.

3.

4.

5.

PROVING A STRENGTH IN AN INTERVIEW

All career positions have requirements that employers are attempting to meet. For example, if you were being considered for a position in a medical laboratory, your course work in chemistry might be the most important strength an employer would seek. If you were interviewing for a position with a volunteer organization, the interviewer would probably be interested in how well you present yourself and the kinds of previous leadership experience you have had. Your analysis of each organization and position available will help you to determine which of your strengths to emphasize. Your goal should be to prove in the interview that your strengths meet the requirements for the job.

There are four distinct steps required for you to prove a strength. The first step takes place prior to the interview; the second, third, and fourth take place during the interview itself.

Step 1—Identify the strength(s) that you believe are most important to the position in question.

> **Example:** In reading over the job announcement posted in the placement office, you have noticed that the organization is looking for applicants with a good advertising background and work experience in the field.

Step 2—Identify the strength you will prove.

> **Example:** "As I researched your company I was able to determine that you are looking for individuals with a strong advertising background, as well as the ability to work with a diverse client group."

Step 3—Describe the background experience you have had that will support or prove your strengths.

> **Example:** "During the last four years I have completed the courses required for the major in advertising and have maintained a 3.2 grade point average. While attending school I have been actively involved in our college's cooperative education/internship program, which has given me an opportunity to gain practical advertising experience."

Step 4—Repeat to the interviewer the strength that you have just identified.

> **Example:** "I've been looking forward to this interview because it appears that the position you have available closely matches my educational background in advertising, my career interest, and the experience I have recently obtained."

To rehearse this four-step procedure, identify a position for which you would like to be interviewed. Research the organization that offers the position. Then follow the four steps, using the space provided to write out how you would word your proof statement.

Step 1 Strengths required in the organization.

Step 2 Identify the strengths you will prove.

Step 3 Describe the background experience you have had that will support your strengths.

Step 4 Repeat to the interviewer the strengths you have just identified.

RESPONDING TO TYPICAL INTERVIEW QUESTIONS

It will be to your advantage to anticipate the questions interviewers typically ask applicants during an interview. You can then write out in advance how you would respond to them. The following 20 questions are examples of those frequently asked by interviewers.

1. Tell me about yourself. Go beyond what you have included on your résumé.
2. Why are you interested in this position? Why are you interested in our organization?
3. Why did you seek an interview with our organization?
4. Why did you choose your particular major and career field?
5. How would you describe yourself to me?
6. What do you think motivates you to put forth your greatest effort?
7. How would you evaluate your success to date?
8. In what way can you make a contribution to our organization?
9. Describe the relationship that should exist between a manager and subordinates.
10. What do you consider to be your strongest and weakest personal qualities?
11. What accomplishments have given you the most satisfaction? Why?
12. What has been your most rewarding educational experience?
13. If you had to do it over again, how would you plan your preparation differently? Why?
14. What major problems have you encountered, and how have you dealt with them?
15. How well do you function under pressure?
16. What are your long-term goals? Where do you plan to be in your career in ten years?
17. Why should my organization offer you a position?
18. What supervisory or leadership roles have you held?
19. Tell me about your extracurricular activities.
20. Which geographic location do you prefer? Why?

Write out how you would respond to these five typical questions.

1. Why are you interested in this position? Specifically, why are you interviewing with our organization?

2. What motivates you to put forth your greatest effort?

3. In what ways can you make a contribution to our organization?

4. How would you describe yourself?

5. What supervisory or leadership roles have you held?

ANTICIPATING AND RESPONDING TO OBJECTIONS

Not only should you be prepared to answer questions during the interview but you should also anticipate objections the interviewer might raise. Forethought allows you to plan a satisfactory response. Objections typically fall into the category of lack of experience, poor academic achievements, unrealistic salary expectations, lack of technical content in educational preparation, and personality issues. There are several strategies for dealing with objections. You can admit to the shortcoming and allow the interview to continue, or you can admit that the objection is true and provide a superior point to counter the objection. You can also turn the objection into a selling point on your behalf. Another technique is to explain why this objection is not critical, as shown by the following examples.

Interviewer states: "Your résumé shows that you have very little work experience."
Your response: "Yes, I agree that I have had little practical experience, but you will notice that I have been involved in a number of on-campus extracurricular and volunteer experiences."

Interviewer states: "On your résumé you indicated that your GPA is only slightly above a C average. We are primarily interested in A and B students."
Your response: "I'll admit my grades are fairly average. While I attended college I worked nearly full-time to support my college expenses."

Interviewer states: "We are looking for a more outgoing person for our sales engineering positions."
Your response: "Let me explain to you why I appear to be more conservative and quiet. I like to be sure that I understand the complete problem before I respond. I like to do my homework to be sure that I am best able to meet the true needs of potential customers."

Identify some objections you might anticipate regarding your candidacy for a particular job. Write out how you would respond if these objections were raised by the interviewer.

Objection 1:

Your response:

Objection 2:

Your response:

Objection 3:

Your response:

Objection 4:

Your response:

Objection 5:

Your response:

Section 2   Preparing for the Experience

PREPARING TO ASK QUESTIONS YOURSELF

The interview should be a two-way process. Not only will you respond to questions but you should be prepared to ask meaningful questions yourself. Remember, you are trying to determine if this is the organization for which you would like to work. Ask about the job environment in which you would be working and about the structure of the organization. Ask specific questions about the job that you would be doing in the organization and the duties you would be performing. Ask the interviewer where you would be located if offered the position, and ask about the size of the organization and promotional opportunities that may be available.

Be careful not to ask questions about salary or benefits until you are offered the job or until the interviewer brings up the subject first. You should not appear more interested in the salary and benefits than in the job itself. You may decrease your chances of being hired if you are unrealistic in your salary expectations. If you ask for too much, the employer may give you no further consideration. If, on the other hand, you ask for too little the employer may doubt your worth; and, if you are hired, you may later be disappointed to discover that you could have received more if you had asked for it. Beginning wages are often standardized by union contract or company policy and are usually explained to the applicant by the time the position is actually offered. Suggestions for types of questions you should avoid in the interview are given in Figure 9.2. Then in the space provided on page 68, write out five questions you would like to ask during the interview.

Figure 9.2

INTERVIEW QUESTION DON'TS

1. Don't ask about hours.
2. Don't ask questions about salary and fringe benefits.
3. Don't ask questions suggesting that you are willing to do only a minimum amount of work.
4. Don't ask questions relating to working overtime or on weekends.
5. Don't ask questions regarding number of sick or vacation days.
6. Don't ask questions relating to length of the lunch hour or scheduled breaks.
7. Don't ask questions that imply that you will be watching the clock.

1.

2.

3.

4.

5.

ACTIVITY 10
Completing a Successful Interview

Purpose: To assist you in developing the skills required to complete a successful job interview.

Planning and preparation prior to the job interview (as outlined in Activity 9) will make you feel more comfortable with the interview process. Advance planning will help you gain confidence in yourself as an applicant and will also help you better to explain who you are and what your capabilities are. Your major responsibility during the actual job interview is to communicate, in a persuasive fashion, how your knowledge, skills, background, and attitude match the requirements of the employer. Figure 10.1 offers a humorous approach to ideas for job-seeking success.

MAKE A GOOD FIRST IMPRESSION

The first 30 seconds of a job interview are usually considered to be the most critical. How you look (your appearance), how you greet the interviewer, your handshake, where you sit, and your opening statement are all important in making a positive first impression. By practicing the following suggestions, you will improve your chances of creating a good first impression.

Appearance

Your appearance conveys information to the interviewer concerning your age, sex, weight, and physical characteristics, as well as a great deal of information about your personality. For example, your hairstyle will be one of the first things the interviewer will notice. Your intent in grooming should be to eliminate objections the interviewer might have and to convey a favorable first impression. A rule of thumb to use in dress and hairstyle is to follow the standard established for the particular business or industry group. When in doubt, lean toward a more conservative dress and hairstyle than you think the interviewer might expect.

Handshake

Different types of handshake carry different messages to the interviewer. A firm handshake conveys warmth and strength. A prolonged handshake is considered to be more intimate than a brief one, but may cause the interviewer to feel uncomfortable. A limp or cold handshake usually indicates aloofness and perhaps an unwillingness on your part to become involved. A general rule of thumb for shaking hands at the beginning of an interview is to allow the interviewer to extend his or her hand first. Shake hands firmly while maintaining eye contact with the interviewer. This gesture will usually help you in establishing an atmosphere of friendliness and mutual respect, initiating your interview in a positive manner.

Physical Seating Arrangement

If you have a choice between a chair across the desk from the interviewer and a chair beside the interviewer's desk, choose the latter. By sitting at the side of the interviewer, you lower the communication barriers created by the desk.

Figure 10.1

---

10 SUREFIRE WAYS TO IMPROVE YOUR CHANCES OF GETTING A TURNDOWN

1. Be shy and reticent, with a lack of self-confidence.
2. Indicate that you are a "window shopper," a candidate who already knows where he or she will probably work, but who just wants to check around in the job market.
3. Indicate that you aren't sure what you want to do.
4. Ask for counseling in the interview.
5. Bring a copy of your senior class project for "show and tell."
6. Have a nervous mannerism such as drumming your fingers on the desk or ending each statement with ". . . you know?"
7. Don't ask any challenging questions. Instead, say things like, "Boy, it really sounds great. I can't think of any questions."
8. Apologize because you didn't have time to read the company's literature in the placement office.
9. Knock on the door to get the interviewer to hurry up with the evaluation he or she is trying to complete on the last candidate.
10. Answer a question with that age-old statement, "I really like working with people."

SOURCE: John L. Lafevre, Director of Human Resources, Caradco, *CPC Annual,* 31st Ed., Vol. 1, 1988–89, p. 40.

HANDLE OPEN-ENDED INTERVIEW QUESTIONS

Commonly an interviewer will ask a very general type of question early in the interview to determine how well you express yourself under pressure and how well you have prepared for the interview. Open-ended questions require more than a yes or no answer. "Tell me about yourself" and "Why would you like to work in our organization?" are examples of questions you should be prepared to answer. An adequate response should include information on your personal background, educational experiences, extracurricular activities, related work experiences, and outside interests. It would be a good idea to write, or at least outline, how you would present an answer to such a general question. However, attempt to avoid sounding like you have rehearsed your answer. Present your story in a well-organized, straightforward manner without fumbling.

KNOW YOUR JOB OBJECTIVE

Before the interview begins, you should have a good idea of what you would like to do within the organization. You should have narrowed down your statement of job objective to one that is consistent with the position(s) available in the employing organization. Your chances of getting the position are much better if you have a good idea of where you are going with your career than if you appear to lack direction. At a major midwestern college, the majority of students who were rejected at initial full-time placement interviews had poorly defined career plans. A sincere interest in the organization, a specific career orientation, a knowledge of why you would like to work with the organization, and a sense of controlled enthusiasm are all very impressive to an interviewer.

DEVELOP AN INTERVIEW PRESENTATION

Another great way to get a head start on the interview process is to prepare a 10- to 15-minute presentation or speech on "Why you should hire me." Divide the presentation into these topics: educational background, related work experience, transferable skills, success indicators, and personality characteristics. Rehearse your presentation in front of a mirror or with a friend. During the interview, look for opportunities to sell the activities and traits you have identified in your presentation. Questions from the interviewer such as "Tell me about yourself," "Why should I hire you?" and "What have you learned in college?" offer you a good opportunity to present your qualifications and background to the interviewer.

In the space provided, write what you would include under each of the major sections of your presentation.

Educational background

Related work experience

Transferable skills (what can you actually do that will benefit them if they employ you?)

Success indicators (leadership positions held, membership in organizations, scholastic and leadership honors)

Personality characteristics and values (your work attitude, your communication skills, your personal attitude, creativity, determination, charisma, and so on)

EMPHASIZE THE POSITIVE

Always try to accent the positive. Emphasize your strong points and remember that the interviewer is looking for a high level of personal energy and enthusiasm. Although you need not bring up past failures and shortcomings, don't try to cover them up or sidestep them either. If the interviewer asks about them, try to explain the circumstances rather than making excuses or blaming others. Remember that the person interviewing is human too and has probably made a few mistakes in the past. You'll create a better impression by being honest and candid.

ASK MEANINGFUL QUESTIONS

Be prepared to ask meaningful questions, particularly if you are not clear about the details of the job, the training program, or other job-related concerns. Don't ask questions just because you think it is expected. Avoid lengthy discussions about benefits and starting salaries. Let the recruiter volunteer that information, or obtain it in a later interview or from available literature.

Occasionally an interviewer will ask you to identify your greatest weakness. When you are asked this type of question, attempt to sidestep it politely by identifying a nonweakness—that is, something that could be viewed as an asset. A nonweakness would be something like "I have a tendency to take my career too seriously" or "I tend to be overly organized" or "Some people consider me to be too generous." Questions such as these are sometimes asked to test the applicant's ability to handle difficult situations.

STAY IN CONTROL

Every interview is different. The interviewer may want to test your ability to handle stress by asking difficult questions that make you feel uncomfortable. Stay calm. If the interviewer attempts to lead you off on a digression, try to redirect the conversation back to you and the interviewing organization. Your time with the interviewer should be as productive as possible. By remaining confident and determined, you will make a good impression on the interviewer.

CLOSE WITH A STRONG SUMMARY

Prepare a closing summary for the interview. Most interviews will have some time limit, so be respectful of the interviewer's time. Do not spoil a favorable interview with an awkward or delayed leave-taking. When it appears that the employer has completed his questioning and you have presented your story, it is time to leave. Provide a verbal summary of why you would like to work for the organization and how your background matches the requirements of the position. Conclude by letting the interviewer know that you are still very much interested in the position. If the employer has not already told you the next step, it is appropriate to close with such questions as "Before we end the interview, could you tell me what the next step is in the employment process?" or "When can I expect to hear from you regarding this position?" Then leave promptly.

CONDUCT A PRACTICE INTERVIEW

With a friend or a staff member from the placement or cooperative education/internship office serving as the interviewer, rehearse the skills you have learned for participating in a successful interview. Videotaping this experience may be very helpful.

Choose a hypothetical organization and position and go all the way through a practice interview. Afterward, ask the interviewer to complete the "Job Interview Evaluation" form provided on page 75. Practice the job interview several times or until you feel comfortable with the process. With each interview, try to improve your rating on items evaluated as "average" or below. The following questions can serve as guidelines for the person who is playing the role of the interviewer.

Interviewer: "I appreciate your coming in today for this interview. I'd like to ask you some questions, but first take a few minutes and describe yourself and your background to me."

Your response:

Interviewer: "Thanks, that's very interesting. Now tell me what it is about your background and training that you believe qualifies you for employment with this organization."

Your response:

Interviewer: "What do you consider to be your major strengths and weaknesses?"

Your response:

Interviewer: "If we were to offer you a position with our organization, where would you see yourself in ten years?"

Your response:

Interviewer: "How do you think your extracurricular activities while in school will help you in the position you are applying for in our organization?"

Your response:

Interviewer: "Summarize for me why you would like to work for this organization."
Your response:

Interviewer: "Now I'd like to know if you have any questions that I might be able to answer."
Your response:

Refer also to Activity 9, which lists 20 questions typically asked during an interview.

JOB INTERVIEW EVALUATION

Rate yourself, or have another person rate you, on the following criteria for conducting a successful job interview.

2—Poor
4—Fair
6—Average
8—Above average
10—Excellent

1. Interview approach (greeting, introduction, handshake, and eye contact)	2	4	6	8	10
2. Awareness/knowledge of the interviewing organization (products, services, history, and background of the organization)	2	4	6	8	10
3. Appearance (hair, grooming, and professional dress)	2	4	6	8	10
4. Self-knowledge (skills, weaknesses, abilities, values, and experience)	2	4	6	8	10
5. Voice (alert, pleasant, enthusiastic, distinct, and expressive)	2	4	6	8	10
6. Body language (facial expressions, gestures, and posture)	2	4	6	8	10
7. Self-confidence (how you project yourself; being natural and at ease)	2	4	6	8	10
8. Interview presentation/delivery (outline of how and why you should be hired; ability to match your skills and background with requirements of the position available)	2	4	6	8	10
9. Questions (quality of questions asked by the interviewee during the interview)	2	4	6	8	10
10. Responses to questions asked (accuracy and appropriateness of responses, poise under pressure, and ability to turn objections into positive points)	2	4	6	8	10
11. Close of the interview (expression of appreciation for interview, sincerity, and questions relating to the next step in the employment process)	2	4	6	8	10

AFTER THE INTERVIEW

Many jobs are won as a result of careful and effective follow-up. As soon as possible after the interview, provide credentials, references, or transcripts that have been requested by the prospective employer. Be sure to write down the name, title, and address of the interviewer. If the employer has requested that you complete and mail an employment application or furnish additional information, carefully follow the instructions if you expect to receive further consideration.

You should always send the interviewer a letter of appreciation for the opportunity to interview. An example of a thank-you letter is given in Figure 10.2. A thank-you letter can reinforce your interest in the organization and send extra details about qualifications that were not presented in the interview.

If you hear nothing for several weeks, you may wish to write or telephone to check the status of your application. (See Figure 5.3 for an example of a follow-up letter.) This type of follow-up is often a key to job-seeking success. Another good idea is to maintain a record of interviews completed. A form similar to the one shown in Figure 10.3 can assist you in keeping track of your interviews.

Figure 10.2 Sample Thank-You Letter

(Sent to the individual who interviewed you for a cooperative education/internship position.)

```
                                        Your address
                                        City, State ZIP code
                                        Current date


        Inside address
        (Direct to individual who interviewed you)

        Dear _____ :

        Thank you for talking with me last (day of week)
        about the (job title) position. The interview was
        very informative. Your description of the position
        and the tour of your organization have increased my
        interest in a cooperative education/internship
        position in your (department name) department.

        I am confident that I can meet the responsibilities
        of (name of position) and make major contributions to
        (name of company).

        If you need any additional information, please do not
        hesitate to contact me. I look forward to hearing
        from you in the near future.

                                    Sincerely,

                                    (your signature)

                                    Typed name
```

Figure 10.3 Record of Interviews Completed

(Make extra copies prior to filling out this form. A separate form is required for each interview.)

Name of interviewing organization: _____

Address and phone number: _____
(street address)

_____
(city, state, and ZIP)

_____
(phone number)

Name of interviewer: _____

Information about the organization: _____

_____

_____

_____

_____

Information about the specific position available: _____

_____

_____

_____

_____

Salary and job location information: _____

_____

_____

_____

_____

What should be done next: _____

_____

_____

_____

_____

Other information: _____

_____

_____

Completing a Successful Interview

ADDITIONAL RESOURCES

American Marketing Association. "The Employment Kit: A Practical Guide to Achieving Success in the Job Market." Chicago: American Marketing Association, 1986.

Beatty, Richard H. *The Five Minute Interview*. New York: Wiley, 1986.

Beatty, Richard H. *The Résumé Kit*. New York: Wiley, 1984.

Biegeleisen, J. I. *Make Your Job Interview a Success*. New York: Arco, 1985.

Block, Deborah Perlmutter. *How to Have a Winning Job Interview*. Lincolnwood, Ill.: VGM Career Horizons, 1987.

Bolles, Richard Nelson. *The 1988 What Color Is Your Parachute?* Berkeley, Calif.: Ten Speed Press, 1988.

Cohen, William A. *The Student's Guide to Finding a Superior Job*. San Diego, Calif.: Slawson Communications, 1987.

College Placement Council, 62 Highland Ave., Bethlehem, PA 18017. The College Placement Council issues an annual publication, which usually includes an article dealing with the preparation of résumés. Your placement or cooperative education/internship office should have copies of the *CPC Annual* available for your use.

Farr, J. Michael. *Job Finding Fast*. Mission Hills, Calif.: Glencoe, 1988.

Fear, Richard A. *The Evaluation Interview*. 3d ed. New York: McGraw-Hill, 1984.

Fortune. New York: Time, Inc., published biweekly.

Jackson, Tom. *Guerrilla Tactics in the Job Market*. Toronto: Bantam Books, 1978.

Moody's Manuals. New York: Moody's Investor Services.

National Commission for Cooperative Education. "Co-op Education: You Earn a Future When You Earn a Degree." National Commission for Cooperative Education, 360 Huntington Ave., Boston, MA 02115-5005. (Write for free copy.)

National Commission for Cooperative Education. "Co-op Education Undergraduate Program Directory." National Commission for Cooperative Education, 360 Huntington Avenue, Boston, MA 02115-5005. (Write for free copy.)

Powell, C. Randall. *Career Planning Today*. Dubuque, Iowa: Kendal/Hunt, 1981.

Sincoff, Michael Z., and Robert S. Goyer. *Interviewing*. New York: Macmillan, 1984.

Smith, Michael Holly. *The Résumé Writer's Handbook*. 2d ed. New York: Barnes and Noble, 1987.

Standard & Poor's Register of Corporations, Directors & Executives. New York: Standard & Poor's Corporation, 1988.

Standard & Poor's Standard Directory of Advertisers. New York: Standard & Poor's Corporation, 1988.

Thomas Register of American Manufacturers. New York: Thomas Publishing, annually.

Developing Your Training Program to Maximize Benefits

The activities contained in this section are intended for use after you have started working in your cooperative education/internship assignment. The major purpose of all the activities in this section is to help you maximize the benefits you derive from your work assignment. The section begins with an activity that helps you to analyze your own expectations and your employer's as they relate to your cooperative education/internship job assignment.

As you start a new job of any type, there are many things that you need to learn about your employer. Activity 12 helps you to analyze your job environment. You will examine policies and procedures in the organization, the organizational structure, and the mission and goals of the organization. This activity concludes with a self-administered questionnaire that will help you to understand the organizational climate in which you are working.

Activity 13 leads you through the process of developing a job description for your cooperative education/internship position. You will also examine the benefits and drawbacks of job descriptions.

Activity 14 is one of the most important you will complete. You will be asked to prepare performance objectives describing tasks and job activities that you would like to accomplish during your cooperative education/internship experience. These performance objectives are critical because in a later activity they will become the basis for your job supervisor's evaluation of your job performance. Preparing performance objectives may not be a new experience for your job supervisor because there is a good chance that the organization where you are employed follows some type of management-by-objectives (MBO) system.

The final activity in this section helps you in identifying nontechnical types of problems that occur in the workplace. A major part of this activity relates to helping you understand your own interpersonal skills, which have an impact on your success on the job.

ACTIVITY 11
Examining Expectations

Purpose: To understand employer and employee expectations and how they affect your success on the job.

In his book *Your Career in the World of Work,* Milton Berlye defines success as, ". . . the release and the fulfillment of the hopes and dreams and the hidden talents that cry out and pound so furiously within the human breast. Success is usually, but not necessarily, associated with the attainment of wealth, favor, or eminence."[1] While you may have your own expectations for the job, your employer also has a set of expectations for you. The degree to which you are able to meet his or her expectations determines how successful you will be.

An employer's expectations include not only the performance of the tasks assigned but also how well you fit in with the other employees and with the organization itself. If you do not seem part of the employer's organization, your chances for raises and promotions will be very slim indeed. Being too different might even affect your ability to hold your job.

In this activity, you will identify employer and employee expectations and discover how they might affect your future. Since one purpose of this book is to help you achieve satisfaction in your career, being successful in each job is an important part of this satisfaction. Berlye defines a career as, ". . . a succession of productive experiences intertwined over a lifetime leading toward a more satisfying life for one's self and others."[2] Let's examine employer and employee expectations.

EMPLOYER EXPECTATIONS

When they offer an applicant a position with the company, employers generally assume that the employee will meet certain expectations. Of course these expectations will vary from employer to employer and from company to company. But some of these expectations are generally accepted to be standard. Employers expect employees to

- adhere to the policies of the organization and to follow instructions;
- be productive and to complete tasks in a reasonable amount of time;
- be loyal to the company;
- show interest and to become involved in company activities;
- have a good attitude and to assume responsibility for regular attendance.

What are some of the expectations that your cooperative education/internship employer might have for you? List at least ten expectations.

1.

2.

---

[1] Milton Berlye, *Your Career in the World of Work* (Indianapolis: H. W. Sams and Company, 1975): 1.
[2] Ibid., p. 1.

3.

4.

5.

6.

7.

8.

9.

10.

You know from observing people in the workplace that some employees do only what a job requires while others always seem to do more than is necessary. (Of course, some employees do less than required, but, in most organizations, they do not last long.) What is it that makes the successful employee stand out? What is it that attracts the attention of the boss?

Here is a list of statements about expectations. You should read each one and place a −, 0, or + beside it. A minus (−) means that you disagree with the statement, a zero (0) indicates you do not know, and a plus (+) means that you agree.

_____ 1. Employers like workers who look for opportunities to do something different.

_____ 2. The best way to get the support you need is to complain when something goes wrong.

_____ 3. Every organization has rules and regulations. You should try to discover what they are and adhere to them.

_____ 4. Most employees spend too much time doing the job they are paid to do.

_____ 5. The typical employee spends 25–30% of his or her time waiting for thanks or a promotion.

_____ 6. Over half of all workers think of themselves as "victims" of the system.

_____ 7. An old-fashioned idea that has outlived its usefulness is the notion of "an honest day's work for a day's pay."

_____ 8. Employers resent employees who are always looking for something to do. You should stretch your tasks to fill the time available.

_____ 9. Keeping yourself in good physical health reduces the amount of time you are absent from the job.

_____ 10. If company practices are unjust, it is your responsibility to see that the other employees are informed.

_____ 11. You get ahead best by making slower co-workers look bad.

_____ 12. An employer should not dictate how you should dress on the job. Today's styles have changed and there is greater freedom of expression.

_____ 13. When you have finished your work, wait for new tasks to be assigned. You don't want to make a pest of yourself by asking for new assignments.

_____ 14. Employers take a negative view of the employee who tries to expand his or her role. Stick to the tasks assigned.

_____ 15. Don't volunteer! The boss will choose the person best suited to the task.

Now score your responses as follows. If you had a + beside numbers 1, 3, 4, 5, 6, and 9, record 2 points for each correct answer. For a minus (−) beside numbers 2, 7, 8, 10, 11, 12, 13, 14, and 15, score 2 points for each correct answer. Zeros count as zero, as do incorrect answers. Add your score and record the total here.

Total Points _____

If your total is 20 or greater, you are probably accurate in assessing employer expectations. Fewer than 20 points means that you need to improve your knowledge in this area. The references at the end of Section 3 will help you get started.

Compare the previous 15 statements about expectations with the list you generated at the beginning of this activity. Were there any similar items? Did you identify the employer expectations correctly? If not, think about your answers and discuss them with your program coordinator/counselor.

EMPLOYEE EXPECTATIONS

Employees also have certain expectations for the job. Many of these expectations are personal; others are job-related. Sometimes these expectations are set too high and can never be achieved. Sometimes the expectations are too low, and the employee never experiences a feeling of accomplishment. Employee expectations should be realistic for each particular job situation.

In general, employees should expect

■ a clear definition of job duties and responsibilities;
■ to receive an employees' manual or handbook that outlines company policies and benefits;
■ to be treated fairly;
■ a clean, comfortable, safe place in which to work;
■ adequate wages and fringe benefits;
■ proper supervision in order to complete tasks safely and efficiently;
■ opportunity to succeed and advance in the company.

What are some of the expectations that you have for your cooperative education/internship position? Try to list at least ten expectations in the space provided.

1.

2.

3.

4.

5.

6.

7.

8.

9.

10.

Look over your list to determine those expectations that are controlled by you and those that are controlled by the company. Divide your list into these two groups:

Controlled by the company:

Controlled by the employee:

Expectations that are controlled by the company are usually set by company policy, but this doesn't mean that an employee cannot change them. By going through the proper channels, employees often initiate changes to existing company policy.

List some opportunities in which an employee might be able to initiate change in company policy.

Committees, special interest groups, special projects, and discussions with supervisors may be some of the items that you have placed on your list. These all offer good opportunities to work toward policy changes.

Now look at your list of expectations that can be controlled by the employee. List some ways to ensure that your expectations are met.

Are working hard, assuming responsibility, and taking initiative on your list? These are generally good ways of achieving expectations on the job.

Compare your list of employer expectations, completed at the beginning of this activity, with your list of employee expectations. Were there any similar items? Do you think that the employer and employee have similar expectations? What can you do in your cooperative education/internship assignment to bring employer and employee expectations closer together? Write a brief paragraph to explain your ideas.

In her book *Skills for Success,* Adele Scheele tells us that most employees spend too much time doing the job assigned; they spend 30% of their time waiting for recognition and, when they don't get it, become resentful. This leads to complaining and, eventually, hostile behavior on the job, resulting in a limited contribution. Employers reward employees who seek work and look for opportunities to contribute. These employees are enriched by expanding their roles and, consequently, becoming more valuable to the organization.[3]

Review the "Ten Keys to Success" shown in Figure 11.1, and follow these guidelines so that you can meet *your* and *your employer's* expectations.

In addition, an employer appreciates an employee who can accept criticism when it is due without becoming hostile and defensive. You will not succeed in every task, but you can learn from your mistakes and keep a positive attitude toward the job. Adele Scheele defines success as, "movement of one step after another," and a career as, "progress through life." "In the most profound sense," she says, "the processes of careering and succeeding must be synonymous."[4]

Figure 11.1

TEN KEYS TO SUCCESS

Dress appropriately.
Discover the rules that govern the job.
Adhere to those rules.
Contribute service for pay received.
Communicate and share ideas.
Develop good habits of attendance and punctuality.
Get along with bosses and co-workers even if they differ from you.
Develop a positive attitude toward the organization.
Be responsible and reliable.
Seek additional tasks and responsibilities.

---

[3] Adele Scheele, *Skills for Success: A Guide to the Top for Men and Women* (New York: Ballantine Books, 1979): 1–8.
[4] Ibid., p. 28.

ACTIVITY 12
Analyzing the Work Environment

Purpose: To help you better understand the environment of your cooperative education/internship work assignment.

As you begin your cooperative education/internship experience, one of your first tasks should be to get acquainted with the organization. You should be familiar with the mission and goals of the organization, the organizational structure, the climate of the organization, and the policies and procedures you are or will be expected to follow.

USEFUL TERMINOLOGY

Before you complete this activity you should know some terminology that is used in nearly all organizations. The following terms will be used throughout this activity, so be sure to study the definitions carefully.

Organization—A group of people working together toward a common purpose or goal.

Formal Organization—The organizational structure created by management to accomplish the purposes or goals of the organization.

Informal Organization—A natural grouping of individuals within an organization based on their needs for companionship, belonging, identity, and personalities, rather than according to a formal plan.

Organizational Climate—The sum of characteristics of the organizational environment, including its strengths and weaknesses. Factors that affect organizational climate include purposes of the organization, structure, leadership, reward structure, strength of relationships, helpful mechanisms, and the organization's attitude toward change.

Organizational Mission—The overall purposes and goals of the organization, or what the organization is all about.

Organizational Chart—A diagram illustrating the formal chain of command or authority structure in an organization. An organizational chart shows by position title who is officially responsible to whom in an organization.

Organizational Manual—A written document that spells out the formal policies, procedures, and rules of an organization.

Policies—Broad or general statements that guide decision making and the behavior of employees in an organization.

Procedures—Specific steps to be followed in implementing policies and accomplishing the purposes or goals of the organization. Procedures stress details and are more specific than policies.

Rules and Regulations—Governing laws in an organization relating to what is considered acceptable conduct or behavior of employees.

ACQUIRING INFORMATION ABOUT THE ORGANIZATION

You can acquire information about the organization by reading available materials, by interviewing other employees, and by observing daily activities.

Reading Formalized Materials

Most organizations make written materials about the organization available to employees. Beginning employees are usually asked to read a policies and procedures manual that applies to the organization as a whole and to the employee's work unit. Many other types of literature should also be on hand in the department, division, or work unit and/or the personnel office, the training department, or, in a larger organization, the company library. Reading matter may include work unit policies and procedures manuals, operating manuals, general personnel policies and procedures manuals, annual reports, product or service manuals, and many other brief pamphlets, brochures, and publications.

Ask your supervisor or manager to help you identify the publications you should be reading during your work assignment. List these suggestions by title in the space provided, together with the date by which you plan to have them read.

Title of Publication	Scheduled Date to Finish Reading
1. _____	_____
2. _____	_____
3. _____	_____
4. _____	_____
5. _____	_____

Interviewing Others

As a cooperative education/internship student you will frequently be asked to interview selected people in your organization in order to complete other assignments in this book. There are two basic ideas you should keep in mind when interviewing others. First, you should try to make the person being interviewed (the interviewee) feel comfortable. For that reason, you should present yourself as openly as possible, explaining the reasons for your interview, what you hope to accomplish, what the information will be used for, and whether the information you collect will be kept confidential. Second, it is important that the interviewee do most of the talking during the interview. You should plan a sufficient number of interview questions and stick closely to those questions during the interview.

To practice your interviewing skills, interview your supervisor or manager. Make the subject for this interview "opportunities for advancement in this organization." Plan the questions you will ask and then record the interviewee's responses in your own words after each question. Make your interview short by limiting your interview to three questions.

Question 1:

Response:

Question 2:

Response:

Question 3:

Response:

Making Observations

You can also learn about your job and what is happening around you by simple observation. Opportunities for informal observation arise continually and contribute to your understanding of the organization and development of your job skills. You can also collect useful information by making more formal types of observation, although the process is somewhat difficult and time consuming. The observer not only has to be at the right place at the right time but must know what to look for and how to record the information. The observer must also be careful not to become a nuisance to those being observed. One of the keys to making meaningful observations is to define exactly what you are looking for and to use an observation form of some type. Figure 12.1 shows a form that can be used to document observations.

MISSION AND GOALS OF THE ORGANIZATION

An **organization** can be defined as a group of people working together toward a common purpose or goal. Some organizations exist to provide a return on investment to their stockholders, and others are organized on a nonprofit basis to deliver needed services to people. Many organizations have developed mission statements. A **mission statement** outlines in simple language what the organization is all about, why it exists, and its basic purposes and goals. Some mission statements are formalized and widely distributed throughout the organization. Others are less formal and perhaps even unwritten. An example of a formal mission statement for a medium-sized financial institution is shown in Figure 12.2.

The organization where you are completing your cooperative education/internship assignment probably has some type of document (a mission statement) that outlines the broad purposes and goals of the organization. If possible, obtain a copy of the document, review it carefully, and then write a summary regarding the mission of the organization. If a written statement does not exist, interview your supervisor or someone from the personnel office to learn what the purposes and goals of the organization are.

In the space provided, summarize the basic purposes of your employing organization. Identify if possible the clientele or customers being served, commitment to people working in the organization, and other elements that make up the mission.

Figure 12.1   Observation Form

Location: _____

Name of observer: _____

Date and time: _____

Planned objectives of observation:

General overview of observation:

Details of observation:

Interpretation (what observations may mean):

Observer's feelings:

Figure 12.2

MISSION STATEMENT FOR AMERICA FIRST CREDIT UNION

Our mission is to provide personal financial services of superior quality to the member/owners; our chief concern being their financial well-being.

We desire to be the primary financial institution of our members. We will use automation and technology to support a highly trained group of volunteers and staff.

Professional managers will be accountable for the quality of service and will be given sufficient flexibility in implementing policy to insure that the members perceive the highest degree of excellence in every contact.

Professional marketing will provide aggressive programs to sustain and increase growth. We will seek our growth both from new members and by serving the financial needs of present members in a more complete manner. We will not sacrifice quality of present services to seek growth.

In order to provide quality member services, the credit union must remain financially sound and secure. Adequate operating controls, capital reserves and liquidity will be maintained at all times.

We will be sales oriented in our approach to members, but traditional credit union philosophy will remain our guiding principle. Among financial institutions, this credit union is a unique organization with deep and abiding human values. Our goal is to maintain those qualities.

SOURCE: America First Credit Union, Ogden, Utah. Reprinted with permission.

LOOKING AT THE FORMAL ORGANIZATIONAL STRUCTURE

Every organization makes use of some type of **organizational chart** to show where and how specific positions and functions fit into the organization and to define the relationships among them. The organizational chart will vary with the size and complexity of the organization. Obtain a copy of the organizational chart for your organization and locate your department, division, or unit within the larger structure. On page 92, headed "Organizational Chart," draw a chart for your department, division, or unit. Be sure you identify your position in the organization. If you work for a smaller enterprise, you may choose to draw a chart for the entire organization, showing where your position fits.

FORMAL AND INFORMAL LEADERS

The organizational chart identifies who officially has the authority or who is the designated leader at each level in the organization. Your supervisor or manager is your designated **formal leader.** Formal leaders have the power to hire, fire, and discipline members of the work group. Their power base is formal. A group's actual leader, however, may be someone other than the designated leader. This person is referred to as the **informal leader.** Informal leaders gain their power by recognizing the needs of the group and then, through cooperation with group members, meeting the needs of the group. Informal leaders may influence employees to either strive for high work performance or restrict performance; to either cooperate or interfere with formal supervision. As you complete your cooperative education/internship assignment, it is important that you be able to

Organizational Chart

recognize who, informally, has the most influence on your work group. Answer the following questions regarding the formal and informal leader in your department, division, or work unit.

1. Who is the designated formal leader in your work unit?

2. What qualities does this person have that positively influence the outcomes of your work group?

3. Whom do you consider to be the informal leader in your work unit?

4. What qualities does this person have that positively influence the outcomes of your work group?

ORGANIZATIONAL CLIMATE

Organizational climate refers to all the elements within an organization that have an impact on how it functions. Climate can be evaluated by developing a profile of selected elements in the organization. A self-administered, self-scored questionnaire can provide you with an estimate of the climate of your organization. The *Organizational Diagnosis Questionnaire* (ODQ) developed by Robert C. Preziosi is a good tool to use.[1] The results will provide you with scores for seven elements that contribute to the organizational climate:

1. Purposes of the organization
2. Structure of the organization
3. Leadership in the organization
4. Rewards provided in the organization
5. Strength of relationships in the organization
6. Helpful mechanisms in the organization
7. The attitude toward change in the organization

Complete the ODQ provided on pages 95 and 96. Follow the directions given at the top and answer each question from your perspective as an employee in the organization. Respond openly and honestly. Then transfer the numbers you circled on the questionnaire to the blanks provided on the ODQ Scoring Sheet on page 97. Add each column and divide each total by 5. This will give you comparable scores for each of the seven elements. Transfer the average scores for each of the seven elements to the ODQ Interpretation Sheet on page 98.

---

[1] Robert C. Preziosi, *Organizational Diagnosis Questionnaire. The 1980 Annual Handbook for Group Facilitators* (San Diego, Calif.: University Associates, 1980).

To interpret your score, read over the description of each of the seven elements on the interpretation sheet. The simplest way of interpreting this information is to calculate the difference between the neutral score of 4 and the average score for each dimension. A score of 4 would mean that the organization is not functioning well on this dimension. The closer the score is to 7, the more severe the problem. Scores lower than 4 indicate that there is no problem. A score of 1 indicates optimal functioning.

After you have completed the three parts of the ODQ, read over the ODQ Interpretation Sheet carefully and then answer the following questions:

1. What are the strongest elements in your organization?

2. What do you think contributes to making these elements areas of strength?

3. What are the weakest elements in your organization?

4. What do you think contributes to making these elements weak?

ORGANIZATIONAL DIAGNOSIS QUESTIONNAIRE

Robert C. Preziosi

From time to time organizations consider it important to analyze themselves. It is necessary to find out from the people who work in the organization what they think if the analysis is going to be of value. This questionnaire will help the organization that you work for analyze itself.

Directions: Do not put your name anywhere on this questionnaire. Please answer all thirty-five questions. *Be open and honest.* For each of the thirty-five statements, circle only *one* (1) number to indicate your thinking.

1—Agree strongly	5—Disagree slightly
2—Agree	6—Disagree
3—Agree slightly	7—Disagree strongly
4—Neutral	

1. The goals of this organization are clearly stated.	1	2	3	4	5	6	7
2. The division of labor of this organization is flexible.	1	2	3	4	5	6	7
3. My immediate supervisor is supportive of my efforts.	1	2	3	4	5	6	7
4. My relationship with my supervisor is a harmonious one.	1	2	3	4	5	6	7
5. My job offers me the opportunity to grow as a person.	1	2	3	4	5	6	7
6. My immediate supervisor has ideas that are helpful to me and my work group.	1	2	3	4	5	6	7
7. This organization is not resistant to change.	1	2	3	4	5	6	7
8. I am personally in agreement with the stated goals of my work unit.	1	2	3	4	5	6	7
9. The division of labor of this organization is conducive to reaching its goals.	1	2	3	4	5	6	7
10. The leadership norms of the organization help its progress.	1	2	3	4	5	6	7
11. I can always talk with someone at work if I have a work-related problem.	1	2	3	4	5	6	7
12. The pay scale and benefits of this organization treat each employee equitably.	1	2	3	4	5	6	7
13. I have the information that I need to do a good job.	1	2	3	4	5	6	7
14. This organization is not introducing enough new policies and procedures.	1	2	3	4	5	6	7
15. I understand the purpose of the organization.	1	2	3	4	5	6	7
16. The manner in which work tasks are divided is a logical one.	1	2	3	4	5	6	7

		1	2	3	4	5	6	7
17.	This organization's leadership efforts result in the organization's fulfillment of its purposes.	1	2	3	4	5	6	7
18.	My relationships with members of my work group are friendly as well as professional.	1	2	3	4	5	6	7
19.	The opportunity for promotion exists in this organization.	1	2	3	4	5	6	7
20.	This organization has adequate mechanisms for binding itself together.	1	2	3	4	5	6	7
21.	This organization favors change.	1	2	3	4	5	6	7
22.	The priorities of this organization are understood by its employees.	1	2	3	4	5	6	7
23.	The structure of my work unit is well designed.	1	2	3	4	5	6	7
24.	It is clear to me whenever my boss is attempting to guide my work efforts.	1	2	3	4	5	6	7
25.	I have established the relationships that I need to do my job properly.	1	2	3	4	5	6	7
26.	The salary that I receive is commensurate with the job that I perform.	1	2	3	4	5	6	7
27.	Other work units are helpful to my work unit whenever assistance is requested.	1	2	3	4	5	6	7
28.	Occasionally I like to change things about my job.	1	2	3	4	5	6	7
29.	I desire less input in deciding my work unit goals.	1	2	3	4	5	6	7
30.	The division of labor of this organization helps its efforts to reach its goals.	1	2	3	4	5	6	7
31.	I understand my boss's efforts to influence me and the other members of the work unit.	1	2	3	4	5	6	7
32.	There is no evidence of unresolved conflict in this organization.	1	2	3	4	5	6	7
33.	All tasks to be accomplished are associated with incentives.	1	2	3	4	5	6	7
34.	This organization's planning and control efforts are helpful to its growth and development.	1	2	3	4	5	6	7
35.	This organization has the ability to change.	1	2	3	4	5	6	7

REPRINTED FROM: J. William Pfeiffer and John E. Jones, *The 1980 Annual Handbook for Group Facilitators.* San Diego, Calif.: University Associates, Inc., 1980. Used with permission.

ODQ SCORING SHEET

Instructions: Transfer the numbers you circled on the questionnaire to the blanks below, add each column, and divide each sum by five. This will give you comparable scores for each of the seven areas.

ELEMENT 1 Purposes	ELEMENT 2 Structure	ELEMENT 3 Leadership	ELEMENT 4 Relationships
1 _____	2 _____	3 _____	4 _____
8 _____	9 _____	10 _____	11 _____
15 _____	16 _____	17 _____	18 _____
22 _____	23 _____	24 _____	25 _____
29 _____	30 _____	31 _____	32 _____
Total _____	Total _____	Total _____	Total _____
Average _____	Average _____	Average _____	Average _____

ELEMENT 5 Rewards	ELEMENT 6 Helpful Mechanisms	ELEMENT 7 Attitude Toward Change
5 _____	6 _____	7 _____
12 _____	13 _____	14 _____
19 _____	20 _____	21 _____
26 _____	27 _____	28 _____
33 _____	34 _____	35 _____
Total _____	Total _____	Total _____
Average _____	Average _____	Average _____

ODQ INTERPRETATION SHEET

Instructions: Transfer the average score from the ODQ Scoring Sheet to each element.

AVERAGE
SCORE:

_____ Element 1: Purposes of the Organization.

How clearly are the mission and goals of the organization stated? Is the mission a clear reflection of what you see going on in the organization? Is it clear why this organization exists? What input do workers have on setting goals for the organization?

_____ Element 2: Structure of the Organization.

How well-structured is the organization? Are formal lines of authority and responsibility clear? How well is work organized so as to reach the goals of the organization?

_____ Element 3: Leadership in the Organization.

How effective is your supervisor in helping your work unit progress toward the overall goals of the organization? Does your supervisor ask for your advice before making a decision?

_____ Element 4: Relationships in the Organization.

How supportive is your supervisor toward what you are doing? How open and effective are communications within the organization? How much conflict exists in the organization?

_____ Element 5: Rewards Provided in the Organization.

Does your current job provide you with a challenge and an opportunity for growth? How equitable are the pay scale and benefits in the organization? Is there a relationship between what is expected in job performance and the reward system?

_____ Element 6: Helpful Mechanisms in the Organization.

How helpful are your immediate supervisor and your co-workers to you in performing your job duties? Do you have the necessary information required to perform your job duties?

_____ Element 7: Attitude of Organization Toward Change.

How open or resistant are the organization and its work force toward change? How free do you feel to make changes in how you go about performing your job duties?

UNDERSTANDING YOUR ORGANIZATION'S POLICIES AND PROCEDURES

Most organizations have a policies and procedures manual to guide decision making and behavior in the organization. Policies are usually general and will not tell you or other employees how to carry out your job responsibilities. A **policy** provides a general framework within which a decision can be made. For example, many organizations have a policy of promoting from within. A **procedure** specifies the steps to be followed in implementing an organizational policy. For example, to implement the policy of promotion from within, an organization might specify a set of procedures for advertising the availability of an open position within the organization prior to announcing the position to outside applicants. Procedures frequently are stated in terms of **rules and regulations,** which guide the behavior of workers in the organization.

Identify three major policies of your organization that affect either you or your work unit. List the procedures that are specified to accomplish the goal of each policy. You might include policies concerning overtime, paid leave, work hours, promotion, personal use of the telephone, equipment, and supplies, performance evaluation, educational leave, quality control, or customer service policies.

Policy 1:

Recommended procedures:

Policy 2:

Recommended procedures:

Policy 3:

Recommended procedures:

ACTIVITY 13
Developing a Job Description

Purpose: To help you develop a better understanding of what constitutes a good job description, as well as the potential benefits and drawbacks of having a job description. To help you develop a high-quality job description for your cooperative education/internship experience.

When you start your cooperative education/internship experience, one of your first assignments should be to determine whether a current and accurate job description exists for your position. If not, it would be beneficial for you, with the aid of your job supervisor, to develop such a document. If one already exists, review the job description carefully for your own understanding and also to determine if it accurately reflects your duties. In either case, when you finish this activity you will have an up-to-date job description for your position.

A **job description** is a statement of a job to be done. A good job description should be a concise one- or two-page summary of the primary job responsibilities and duties, as well as the qualifications for the position. Information for a job description is obtained by performing a job analysis. A **job analysis** is the process of determining the requirements of a job and the qualifications (knowledge, skills, and attitudes) of the person to be placed in that job. Information for the job analysis can be obtained from various sources, including interviews, position questionnaires, and observation. Many different formats are used; however, job descriptions usually include the following elements:

- Job title
- General description of position
- Qualifications (education and experience requirements)
- Lines of promotion (positions that may be available to you should you be promoted)
- Reporting structure (job title of the person to whom you report)

Figure 13.1 contains a sample job description for a management trainee position.

BENEFITS AND DRAWBACKS OF JOB DESCRIPTIONS

Job descriptions should not be disorganized summaries or overly complicated explanations of job responsibilities. Instead, they should provide the worker with a picture of the job and its major responsibilities.

Job descriptions can have both positive and negative value for management and employees. Some of the benefits of job descriptions include the following.

1. They provide a quick orientation of the new employee to the responsibilities of the job.
2. They help to eliminate potential misunderstandings among employees functioning within the same organizational unit.
3. They help to stimulate communication between employees and management regarding the detailed responsibilities of a given position.
4. They can serve as a basis for the establishment of performance evaluation standards for a particular position.

Figure 13.1   Sample Job Description

Job Title: Management Trainee

General Description of Position:

The position of management trainee has been established to attract and retain persons who possess management potential but lack the necessary retail experience. The objective of this job is to train employees for management responsibility. The trainee will undergo extensive on-the-job training designed to provide a working knowledge of technical skills necessary for promotion.

Special Job Responsibilities:

The management trainee's duties may range from relatively simple stock work to more advanced managerial assignments. The trainee will perform the job assigned to him/her and will observe all aspects of operations and merchandising in order to prepare for promotion. Assignments to this position will be limited to four months. During this time, frequent performance reviews, both oral and written, will be completed by the manager. These reviews must be approved by the district director. If, at the end of a maximum of four months, the trainee is not ready to accept an assignment, s/he shall be dropped from the program. The management trainee must be able to relocate.

Qualifications:

Education Required: One year of college or equivalent business experience.

Experience Required: Retail work experience preferred.

Lines of Promotion:

Assistant store manager, store manager, and district manager.

Reporting Structure:

Store manager or assistant manager.

Date Job Description Revised:

6/89

5. They can serve as a partial basis for the evaluation of employee performance on the job.
6. They help to clarify job expectations.

Although job descriptions are generally seen as beneficial to the organization, they also have a few potential drawbacks.

1. Occasionally they may limit the employee to performing only those duties listed in the job description; they may discourage creativity and initiative.
2. Poorly written or inaccurate job descriptions can result in disagreement between management and the employee who assumes that the job description outlines job responsibilities.
3. Most jobs are dynamic and constantly changing. Job descriptions have a tendency to become outdated, and then any evaluation based on their content may be invalid.
4. They can be overused by management rather than used as a tool in conjunction with other available information.

DETERMINING IF A JOB DESCRIPTION EXISTS FOR YOUR POSITION

Cooperative education/internship employers may or may not have developed specific job descriptions for co-op/internship positions. As a co-op/internship student, you may be expected to work within an existing job description, or you may need to develop a new one.

Does a job description exist for your cooperative education/internship position?

Yes _____ No _____

Exact job title: _____

Date this job description was initially developed: _____

Date this job description was last revised: _____

If there is no up-to-date job description for your position, continue reading and working the activities under "Developing a Job Description." You should then read the section "Evaluating an Existing Job Description," but *do not* complete the activities in that section.

If an up-to-date job description already exists for your position, read through the section "Developing a Job Description," but *do not* complete the activities. Once you are familiar with the process, move on to "Evaluating an Existing Job Description" and work the activities in that section.

DEVELOPING A JOB DESCRIPTION

An accurate job description cannot be developed overnight. There are four steps you should follow in developing one. Of course, as you go through this process, you will want to work with your job supervisor to ensure that your description accurately reflects the requirements of your job.

Complete a Weekly List of Job Responsibilities

Complete the "Weekly Job Responsibilities" form (page 105) during the next two weeks. Record all the specific responsibilities you have each day. At the end of the two-week period, review the information with your job supervisor to determine if you have omitted any specific responsibilities. List them on the back of the form. Then prepare the "Summary of Job Responsibilities" (on page 107).

WEEKLY JOB RESPONSIBILITIES

Job responsibilities   Monday   Date _____

Job responsibilities   Tuesday   Date _____

Job responsibilities   Wednesday   Date _____

Job responsibilities   Thursday   Date _____

Job responsibilities   Friday   Date _____

Job responsibilities   Monday   Date _____

Job responsibilities   Tuesday   Date _____

Job responsibilities   Wednesday   Date _____

Job responsibilities   Thursday   Date _____

Job responsibilities   Friday   Date _____

SUMMARY OF JOB RESPONSIBILITIES

1.

2.

3.

4.

5.

6.

7.

8.

9.

10.

Locate Your Job Title in the DOT

Refer to the *Dictionary of Occupational Titles* (DOT), published by the U.S. Department of Labor. Revised approximately every ten years, the DOT is available in nearly all public and college libraries. Volume I of the fourth edition of the DOT (1977) contains job definitions and descriptions for nearly 20,000 different jobs. In 1986 a supplement was published that contains information on 300 new jobs, most of which were high-tech positions.

Using the DOT or the supplement, locate a position similar to yours. Refer to the alphabetical index of occupational titles (page 965 of the DOT). Then, on the basis of the nine-digit code, identify the job title that most closely corresponds to your position. For example, let's say that the title for your cooperative education/internship position is management trainee. In the alphabetical index, this title is listed with a nine-digit code of 189.167-018. You can then easily locate the position title and corresponding description on page 138 of the DOT. Figure 13.2 provides the complete reference and description for this job title.

Figure 13.2

189.167-018   MANAGEMENT TRAINEE (any ind.)

Performs assigned duties, under close direction of experienced personnel, to gain knowledge and experience required for promotion to management positions: Receives training and performs duties in departments, such as credit, customer relations, accounting, or sales to become familiar with line and staff functions and operations and management viewpoints and policies that affect each phase of business. Observes and studies techniques and traits of experienced workers in order to acquire knowledge of methods, procedures, and standards required for performance of departmental duties. Workers are usually trained in functions and operations of related or allied departments to facilitate transferability between departments and to provide greater promotional opportunities.

SOURCE: U.S. Department of Labor, Employment and Training Administration, *Dictionary of Occupational Titles,* 4th ed. (Washington, D.C.: U.S. Government Printing Office, 1977) p. 138.

The first three digits of the nine-digit code classify the position into occupational categories and subcategories. There are nine major categories, which are identified by the first digit.

1. Professional, technical, and managerial occupations
2. Clerical and sales occupations
3. Service occupations
4. Agriculture, fishery, forestry, and related occupations
5. Professional occupations
6. Machine trade occupations
7. Bench work occupations
8. Structural work occupations
9. Miscellaneous occupations

The second three digits of the DOT code indicate the degree of difficulty of the job. Every job requires a worker to function to some degree of difficulty in relation to data, people, and things. The varying degrees of difficulty with respect to data, people, and things are shown in Figure 13.3. The second three digits for the management trainee position are 167. This means that a person in this position would be responsible for coordinating information (data), communicating extensively

Figure 13.3

Data (4th Digit)	People (5th Digit)	Things (6th Digit)
0 Synthesizing	0 Monitoring	0 Setting-up
① Coordinating	1 Negotiating	1 Precision Working
2 Analyzing	2 Instructing	2 Operating–Controlling
3 Compiling	3 Supervising	3 Driving–Operating
4 Computing	4 Diverting	4 Manipulating
5 Copying	5 Persuading	5 Tending
6 Comparing	⑥ Speaking–Signaling	6 Feeding–Offbearing
	7 Serving	⑦ Handling
	8 Taking Instructions–Helping	

with others (speaking–signaling), and handling things (such as materials, supplies, or merchandise) on the job.

The last three digits of the code are used to differentiate the alphabetical order of occupations that have the same first six digits. If the first six digits apply to only one occupation, the last three digits will always be 010.

Please use the *Dictionary of Occupation Titles* to answer the following questions:

1. What is the DOT job title that most closely corresponds to your position? _____

2. What is the nine-digit code that is assigned to this position? _____

After reading the job description provided in the DOT for your position or a similar position, identify at least six major job responsibilities for this position.

1.

2.

3.

4.

5.

6.

What are the second three digits of the nine-digit code assigned to your position? _____

What is your interpretation of these middle three digits in relation to your actual job?

Data:

People:

Things:

Prepare a Draft of Your Job Description

Now that you have some understanding of what constitutes a good job description, you should be ready to develop your own. Prepare a draft of your new job description from the information you have recorded in your "Weekly Job Responsibilities" form and from the information you have reviewed in the *Dictionary of Occupational Titles*. Use the form "Draft for Job Description" on page 113 to complete a draft of your new job description.

Finalize Your Job Description

The first draft of your job description should be used as a basis for further research and discussion before a final job description is developed. Review this first-draft job description with your job supervisor. Make any changes suggested by your job supervisor and then prepare a final draft on the form "Final Job Description" provided on page 115.

DRAFT FOR JOB DESCRIPTION

Job title: _____

General paragraph description of your cooperative education/internship job:

Listing of specific responsibilities:

Qualifications:

Educational

Work experience background

Reporting structure:

Lines of promotion (promotional opportunities):

FINAL JOB DESCRIPTION

Job title: _____

General paragraph description of your cooperative education/internship position:

Listing of specific responsibilities:

Qualifications:

Educational

Work experience

Reporting structure:

Line of promotion (promotional opportunities):

EVALUATING AN EXISTING JOB DESCRIPTION

When you begin your co-op/internship work assignment, there may be an existing job description for your position. If the job description is out of date or incomplete, you will need to revise and perhaps add to it. In that case, review all the duties and responsibilities listed on your job description, discuss them with your job supervisor, and make out a new list of major job responsibilities. Next, use the "Draft for Job Description" form on page 113 to prepare a new draft of your job description. Review this draft again with your job supervisor and rewrite it on the "Final Job Description" form on page 115.

INTERPRETING YOUR JOB DESCRIPTION

After job descriptions are developed or revised, they are likely to be filed and not revised again until it is time for a change in personnel or a performance evaluation. To make better use of your job description, review each of your finalized listings of job responsibilities with your job supervisor. Ask your job supervisor to help you rate the importance of each of your responsibilities according to the following rating scale.

4—Critical
3—Very important
2—Less important
1—Unimportant
0—Should be removed from job description

Job Responsibilities

_____ 1.

_____ 2.

_____ 3.

_____ 4.

_____ 5.

_____ 6.

_____ 7.

_____ 8.

_____ 9.

_____ 10.

In summary, please answer the following questions regarding your job description:

1. Why is a job description important to you as a cooperative education/internship student?

2. How does the organization where you are working keep job descriptions accurate and up to date?

3. How does the organization where you are working use job descriptions in the organization?

4. What does your job supervisor see as the major advantages of having a job description?

ACTIVITY 14
Developing Performance Objectives for Your Job

Purpose: To assist you in developing performance objectives for each cooperative education/internship work assignment period. These objectives should be acceptable to you, your job supervisor, and your program coordinator.

As a cooperative education/internship student you should be interested in learning as much as you can about your job. Your goal should be to maximize the value of your experience. You should be interested in meeting or exceeding your job supervisor's expectations. Preparing performance objectives for each cooperative education/internship work assignment period will assist you in being successful in your job and will help ensure that you learn as much as possible. Of course, at the conclusion of your work assignment, you also want to receive a good evaluation for your efforts, so setting realistic and meaningful performance objectives is important to you.

Performance objectives are job-related objectives you establish with the help of your job supervisor. They relate directly to your job assignment and represent statements concerning routine and specialized job functions that you will be performing during the work period. Additionally they represent your intention to improve your job performance.

Many organizations require employees to establish performance objectives as part of the organization's management-by-objectives system. **Management by objectives** (MBO) is a system that involves setting objectives at every level of the organization, starting at the top. Employees typically establish performance objectives one or two times each year. Then annually, or sometimes semiannually, these objectives will be used by management as the basis for the performance evaluation of employees.

Before you continue with this activity, you should check with your supervisor to determine if your organization uses performance objectives or management by objectives. If some type of MBO system is used in your organization, the established process should be extremely helpful as you complete the remainder of this activity. Answer the following questions after your discussion with your job supervisor.

1. Does your organization require employees to establish performance objectives?

    Yes _____   No _____

2. If yes, how many times each year are performance objectives established? _____

3. What is the procedure followed by employees in your organization in setting performance objectives? (Please describe the steps in the process.)

    a.

    b.

    c.

    d.

    e.

4. What does your job supervisor see as the advantages and disadvantages of having employees develop performance objectives? (Please list three of each.)

   Advantages:

   a.

   b.

   c.

   Disadvantages:

   a.

   b.

   c.

5. How are the performance objectives established by employees tied into the performance evaluation process? (Please describe.)

CATEGORIES OF PERFORMANCE OBJECTIVES

The performance objectives that you establish for each work assignment period will be used in Activity 17, "Evaluating Your Job Performance," to measure your degree of accomplishment against the performance objectives you have established. In this process you can expand your learning opportunities on the job, gain constructive feedback on your performance, set goals for your future, and develop yourself to the fullest extent possible.

Performance objectives for each cooperative education/internship training period usually fall into five categories:

Routine Duties—Improving your performance in day-to-day job functions and activities. (Example: Increasing your efficiency in performing particular job functions you are expected to perform.)

Problem Solving—Solving specific problems in your job area with measurable results. (Example: Equipment you work with is breaking down too frequently and you suggest a solution through an improved maintenance procedure.)

New Skills and Assignments—Learning a new job skill, increasing your knowledge and usefulness, or starting a new assignment on the job. (Example: Learning how to set up a new piece of equipment from instructions provided in an operating manual.)

Personal Improvement—Developing interpersonal skills, improving communication skills, or developing other social skills that will permit you to function more effectively in the work environment. (Example: Developing more effective listening skills when communicating with co-workers.)

Creative Opportunities—Trying new approaches, showing initiative, or having new ideas relative to your work assignment. (Example: Doing some research on a specific job problem after work hours and bringing a possible new idea back to the workplace.)

GUIDELINES FOR PREPARING PERFORMANCE OBJECTIVES

During each cooperative education/internship assignment training period you will be expected to develop new performance objectives. If you will be completing only one work assignment period, you will go through this process once. If, however, you are involved in a cooperative education/internship program with multiple work assignment periods, you will complete this process each time. As you think about specific performance objectives that you might wish to accomplish, keep the following guidelines in mind:

1. The performance objectives you develop should be realistic and achievable within your cooperative education/internship training period. You should have a reasonable chance of accomplishing these performance objectives on your job during the work experience training period.
2. The performance objectives you develop should be as specific as possible so that they can be evaluated (measured) at the end of the cooperative education/internship training period. (Remember, a major portion of your job supervisor's evaluation will be based on the performance objectives you develop.)
3. The performance objectives you establish should be related directly to your job assignment and fall within the limits of your job description.
4. Before you begin working on any of your performance objectives, you should be sure that they have been approved by your job supervisor.
5. As you prepare performance objectives you should select the appropriate language (words) that will communicate effectively to those involved in the process. Here are some words to *avoid:*

   - know
   - understand

   - appreciate
   - enjoy

   - believe
   - learn

   - write
   - select
   - apply
   - assemble
   - reduce
   - compose
   - collect

   - recite
   - compare
   - revise
   - investigate
   - design
   - display
   - deliver

   - contrast
   - develop
   - install
   - create
   - perform
   - plan
   - train

6. Each performance objective you establish should answer the following four key questions. (See the sample performance objectives provided in Figure 14.1.)

   a. What is the task to be accomplished?

   b. How will it be accomplished?

   c. How will it be measured/evaluated and by whom?

   d. When will it be completed?

PREPARING YOUR PERFORMANCE OBJECTIVES

Preparing performance objectives requires that you go through a five-step process, illustrated by the flowchart in Figure 14.2. This process is designed to help you establish meaningful performance objectives and gain your job supervisor's approval of them. You should work cooperatively with your job supervisor to gain as much of his or her input during the process as possible. You may also want to seek the help of your program coordinator. Although you will be requested to develop six finalized performance objectives in this activity, six is not necessarily a magic number. You may develop more or fewer objectives if your job supervisor agrees.

Figure 14.1

SAMPLES OF PERFORMANCE OBJECTIVES

By March 15th [*when*] I will be able to execute the word processing program on the IBM®* personal computer [*what*] by attending two IBM-sponsored classes [*how*] and receiving a certificate of completion [*evaluate*].

By June 3rd [*when*] I will develop a 95% (currently 90%) operating index that is desirable by bank standards [*what*] by determining and encouraging more effective staff utilization [*how*]. My job supervisor will evaluate by comparing monthly computer printouts and reporting on operating index [*evaluate*].

By March 23rd [*when*] I will develop practical working skills in the operation of the microfilm camera [*what*] by receiving instruction from my supervisor, by reading the instruction manual, and by observing expert operators [*how*]. I will demonstrate my skill in all operations of the camera, including cleaning, loading, and maintaining, to my job supervisor [*evaluate*].

By May 4th [*when*] I will devise, print, and post a safety checklist [*what*] using OSHA guidelines, printed information in the office, and supervisor consultations [*how*]. It will be evaluated by the supervisors in each department [*evaluate*] and then posted.

By April 3rd [*when*] I will create a test fixture to run life tests on hot-gas valve fixtures to test for electromechanical reliability [*what*] by examining the present procedure and the steps involved [*how*]. The effectiveness of the test fixture will be compared with that of present methods. My job supervisor will evaluate the fixture through observations and testing [*evaluate*].

By January 23rd [*when*] I will increase sales by 10% [*what*] by selling related products, by developing increased product knowledge, and by studying various sales-oriented manuals and books [*how*]. I will gather sales data and present it to my supervisor for evaluation [*evaluate*].

* IBM is a registered trademark of International Business Machines Corporation.

Step 1: Develop Preliminary Objectives

Review the job description you developed in Activity 13. In the space provided, list six specific objectives you would like to accomplish during this training period. Make sure that the objectives fall within the limits of your job description and that they are attainable. Attempt to define tasks you would like to do better, new procedures you would like to learn, and skills you would like to improve in your job performance. Don't worry about the exact wording of these preliminary performance objectives.

1.

2.

3.

4.

Figure 14.2

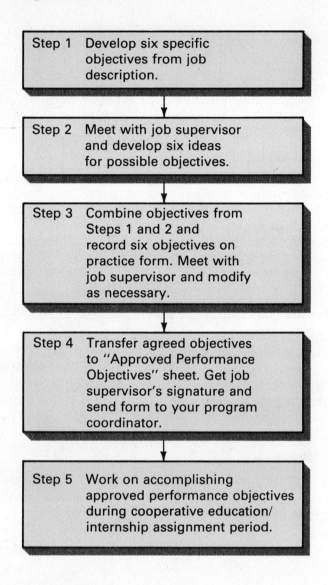

5.

6.

Step 2: Obtain Job Supervisor's Suggestions

Collect ideas from your job supervisor concerning what he or she would like to see you accomplish. Ask your job supervisor to suggest six specific objectives for you to accomplish during this cooperative education/internship training period. List these suggestions here.

1.

2.

3.

4.

5.

6.

Step 3: Combine Objectives

Combine the objectives you listed in Step 1 with the suggestions made by your job supervisor in Step 2. Develop, in sentence form, at least six performance objectives that describe the activity or activities you expect to carry out during your cooperative education/internship work experience. Remember to answer the four key questions (when, what, how, and evaluate) in each of your objectives. Record these performance objectives on the "Practice Sheet for Performance Objectives" on page 125. Review these preliminary performance objectives with your job supervisor and make any changes or modifications agreed to by you and your supervisor.

Step 4: Complete Performance Objectives Sheet

When you and your job supervisor have reached agreement, transfer your finished performance objectives to the "Approved Performance Objectives" sheet on page 127. Ask your job supervisor to sign it as evidence of approval. Send a copy of the approved performance objectives to your college co-op/internship coordinator. Remember, the performance objectives you establish in this activity will be the basis for your job supervisor's evaluation of your performance at the conclusion of the cooperative education/internship period.

Step 5: Accomplish Objectives

Begin working on accomplishing your performance objectives. If it appears that a performance objective is unreasonable or its accomplishment is impossible for some reason beyond your control, you should meet with your job supervisor to adjust your objectives.

PRACTICE SHEET FOR PERFORMANCE OBJECTIVES

(Instructions: The performance objectives you prepare need to be understandable, challenging, specific, measurable, and attainable in the allotted time.)

Performance Objective 1:

Target date for accomplishing objective: _____

Performance Objective 2:

Target date for accomplishing objective: _____

Performance Objective 3:

Target date for accomplishing objective: _____

Performance Objective 4:

Target date for accomplishing objective: _____

Performance Objective 5:

Target date for accomplishing objective: _____

Performance Objective 6:

Target date for accomplishing objective: _____

Cooperative/internship student's name _____

Employing organization _____ Date _____

APPROVED PERFORMANCE OBJECTIVES

(Instructions: Record your approved performance objectives on this sheet. Be sure to review these again with your job supervisor and obtain his or her signature. Then send a copy of these approved performance objectives to your college co-op/internship coordinator.)

1.

2.

3.

4.

5.

6.

_____ Supervisor's signature

ACTIVITY 15
Developing Work Adjustment Skills

Purpose: To help you recognize problems related to work adjust-
ment and to provide strategies for developing adjustment skills.

In Activity 14 you learned about performance objectives, and in Activity 11 you examined employers' expectations. But what happens when your expectations or those of your job supervisor are
not met? Suppose, for example, that your job doesn't provide the kind of satisfaction you expected
and that your motivation to do a good job is declining. Might this circumstance affect your job
performance? Of course it could. Perhaps it already has.

There are many reasons why a job that once seemed like a good choice becomes problem laden
over time. In an exciting article in the 1987 *CPC Annual,* Arthur Miller, Jr., states, "Careers which
can be exciting and productive and deeply fulfilling become stressful and boring and meaningless."
He refers to this condition as **job mismatch.** Job mismatch can result from focusing mainly on work
related to your major field of study, rather than considering how the job allows you to satisfy
values that are important to you, as discussed in Activity 1. Perhaps you have allowed your
employer to define your values for you—to make you into something you are not. Miller reminds
us that "This myth [that we should become what the job needs] is responsible for a sea of wrecked
careers. Believing that I can become what the job needs drives much unhealthy ambition to 'get
ahead.' "[1]

Most of us imagine that there is an ideal job, if only we can find it. In truth, almost any job can
be close to the ideal one if it contains those elements that make a person satisfied and happy. If the
job you have is less than ideal, ask yourself why. Then begin to analyze it in terms of what you
know about yourself from Activity 1. If the problem is not a case of mismatch, then you might find
the solution in one of the following sections.

In general, adjustment problems on the job can be caused by yourself, by other people, or by
the job environment. You could be creating your own problems by the way you approach your
daily tasks. In this case, some assistance with managing time and tasks might be helpful. Sometimes problems grow out of your contact with supervisors and co-workers—human relations
problems. In these instances, it might be worthwhile to work on some basic interpersonal and
communication skills.

On the other hand, your dissatisfaction could result from the environment in which you work.
These job-related factors could be content oriented (having to do with the nature of the tasks) or
organization oriented (having to do with structure, policies, and rules). Each of these categories
warrants examination in some detail.

MANAGING TIME AND TASKS

In *How to Get Control of Your Time and Your Life,* Alan Lakein claims that most people waste 80
percent of their time. They may be attempting to do too many unimportant things, or may not

---

[1] Arthur F. Miller, Jr., "Discover Your Design," *CPC Annual* (Bethlehem, Pa.: College Placement Council, 1987): 2.

really be organized, or may not be working toward specified goals. Whatever the reason, Lakein reminds us that "we all must live on 168 hours a week," and "that's plenty of time to do everything we want to do."[2]

Wasting time can also take the form of procrastination—putting things off. William Knaus, a well-known author on procrastination, describes three causes for it. The first is self-doubt. When you are not confident of your ability you tend to hesitate before acting. The second reason is something Knaus calls "frustration tolerance." People don't want to hassle themselves: "Their real priority in life is being comfortable." If you don't respond to the challenge, you do not risk failure or discomfort. The third cause he cites is poor problem-solving skills. Some people simply haven't developed the ability to handle the challenges that come their way. He adds that perfectionism can lead to procrastination because the self-set standards are so high that one couldn't possibly succeed.[3]

What are the things that waste your time? Think of a job you've had, or your college experience, or a volunteer activity in which you were involved. In the space provided, try to list your top ten time wasters.

1.

2.

3.

4.

5.

6.

7.

8.

9.

10.

A typical list compiled by cooperative education students includes the following 14 items. How many were on your list too? Compare this list with yours and add others that apply to you.

- Being disorganized
- Spending too much time on personal phone calls
- Paying little attention to deadlines
- Procrastinating
- Not understanding instructions
- Having a cluttered work area
- Focusing on detail and not on the "big picture"
- Having to repeat tasks because of inaccuracies
- Trying to do too much in time available

---

[2] Alan Lakein, *How to Get Control of Your Time and Your Life* (New York: Signet, 1973): 13.
[3] William Knaus, "Why People Procrastinate—Is There a Cure?" *U.S. News and World Report* (October 24, 1983): 61.

- Waiting for next assignment without using initiative
- Not knowing where (or when) to begin
- Letting others involve you in their tasks and not completing your own (not saying no)
- Getting bogged down on one task and not moving on to others
- Getting involved in internal politics and not paying attention to business

Recognizing time wasters goes halfway toward solving the problem. You now know what needs work. However, a few other tips might prove helpful.

1. Plan your day's work and try to stick to the plan.
2. Divide large tasks into small, manageable pieces.
3. Reward yourself when a difficult or unpleasant task is completed.
4. Try to concentrate on one project at a time.
5. Set deadlines for yourself.
6. Don't put off tasks that you find unpleasant.
7. Learn to say no to unreasonable requests from co-workers.
8. Try to do first things first.

You can often avoid wasting time by focusing on the task. Instead of feeling that you need more time, concentrate on getting the task done in the time available. Ask yourself questions such as these:

1. What do I need to complete this task?
2. How might it be divided into smaller tasks?
3. What are the parts of this task that should go smoothly?
4. Where might I encounter difficulty?
5. Who can help?
6. What will it look like when it is completed?
7. What are the competing demands on my time?
8. Where should I begin?

Attention to details of time and task management can pay off in reduced anxiety, increased productivity, and more satisfaction from your job. Remember, time management doesn't mean working to fill the time. It means completing projects and having time for leisure activities. In the long run, effective management of time leads to less fatigue and better health, both physically and mentally.

HUMAN RELATIONS ON THE JOB

In getting along with other people, whether professionally or personally, a basic skill is the ability to communicate. It involves your facility for making your needs and feelings known to others (sending) and your receptiveness when others try to share with you (receiving). However, communication is more than sending and receiving messages. Figure 15.1 illustrates other obstacles that can hinder effective communication (filters and negative feedback). The negative effects of filters can be reduced by engaging in clarification procedures called *positive feedback*. The filters shown (tone of voice, attitude, language used, special words) are only some of the things that can cause a message to be misunderstood. There are many other filters, both verbal and nonverbal, that prevent two people from understanding each other.

Negative feedback is a special condition that can create a wall making communication virtually impossible. An example of negative feedback would be hostility on the part of the receiver—an unwillingness to listen to the message. Other examples would be the presence of hidden agendas, defensiveness, stereotyping, and emotional blocks of various kinds. It would be difficult for a message to penetrate those roadblocks.

Positive feedback, on the other hand, allows for both the receiver and the sender to ask and answer questions designed to clarify the message. The result is that the message received is identical to the message being sent. Both parties are thus operating on the same understanding of the communication. You should constantly watch for obstacles in communicating and work on their solutions.

Developing Work Adjustment Skills

Figure 15.1

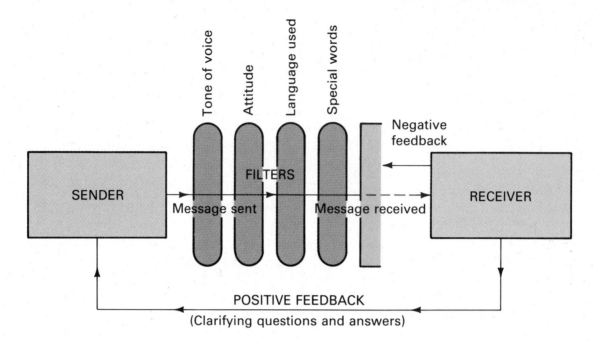

What are some of the obstacles to communication that you have witnessed? List at least five.

1.

2.

3.

4.

5.

What could you do to lessen the effect of each of these obstacles? Use a separate piece of paper to answer this question.

One of the essentials to effective communication is care in sending your message. Try to avoid using terms or words whose meaning may not be generally understood. Use language that is clear and precise, and be articulate. Develop a tone of voice that is pleasing, yet assertive. Don't let your nonverbal behavior conflict with your verbal message. Develop a style of communication that does not promote a defensive reaction from the receiver. Ask questions to test how your message is being received. Above all, practice communicating, both orally and in writing.

Just as important to the communication process as the ability to send messages is the ability to receive them. As Figure 15.1 shows, it is incumbent upon the receiver not to produce roadblocks (negative conditions) and to attempt to understand what is being transmitted. In order to understand what is being sent, the receiver must develop good listening skills. Listening is more than hearing what is said. It requires conscious activity on the part of the listener. One must choose to listen. There must be a desire to understand the message, to focus attention on it, to clarify, and to react to it. The receiver must avoid interrupting, should attempt to block out distractions, and should delay evaluation of the message until the sender has finished. Success on the job may depend to a large degree on how well you listen. Work to develop good listening skills.

Working in groups is also an exercise in human relations. One of the challenges attending the transition from school to work is the need to recognize that the rules for success have changed. In school, your success is determined largely by the individual effort you put forth. You are evaluated singly on assignments and tests. Your papers, projects, and reports are normally independent activities, rarely group efforts. Your grades are personal and specific and are identified with you. Finally, you receive an individual diploma, accompanied, perhaps, by honors you yourself have earned.

Success is measured differently in the workplace. Although individual effort is important, success is often determined by how well a team, group, or department performs in given tasks. It is not the ability to compete that is rewarded but the ability to cooperate. A *team* is graded, not its individual members. Individual contributions may not even be noted. Likewise, when individual tasks are assigned, there is a different kind of deadline imposed. It is not the deadline of term grades but a deadline dictated by organizational or customer needs.

This concept is far different from the process you are accustomed to in school and requires a major readjustment. Amid all the benefits of having work experience in the curriculum to enhance academic learning by introducing practical applications, this lesson is the one most often overlooked.

Have you ever been in a position in which cooperation was more important than competition with members of your group? Have you played on a team, either in sports, in student activities, or in a volunteer activity? Choose one instance when you have been part of a team having a specific task. On a separate piece of paper, describe that group, its tasks, and your particular role. Focus especially on why cooperation among members was so important for success. What kind of reward system was used to ensure success? When you have finished this assignment, examine your description for ways to improve cooperation.

COPING WITH STRESS

In the preface to his book *Coping with Job Stress,* Herbert Greenberg says, "Job stress is no longer considered the sole prerogative of the top executive or the busy air controller. We now recognize that all work requires stress, that all jobs produce stress."[4] Hans Selye, a leading authority on stress and its effects, reminds us that stress is not a negative condition. Stress is a necessary ingredient for stimulating productivity. It is when stress becomes distress, when the stressors produce negative results, that problems occur.

Of course, not all stressors come from the work environment. Much stress is caused by ordinary life events, such as breakup of a relationship, death of a parent, loss of a job, or serious illness. An interesting checklist for measuring the effects of life events on level of stress is the *Social Readjustment Rating Scale,* developed by Holmes and Rahe. If you would like to explore this subject in more detail, see the list of additional resources at the end of Section 3. Selye and others point out that serious illness may arise from stress-related causes.

Occupational stress, however, is a condition resulting from factors in the workplace. Many of the more recent studies have demonstrated that job stress results from these conditions:

- Having too much, or too little, to do
- Having responsibility without concomitant authority
- Having little or no input into decisions that affect you
- Receiving ambiguous or vague instructions
- Receiving conflicting demands from superiors
- Being responsible for the lives and/or the careers of others

These stressors affect all workers, regardless of their level within the organizational hierarchy. Yet many people who work under seemingly stressful conditions are unaffected by them or even thrive on them. How can this be?

---

[4] Herbert M. Greenberg, *Coping with Job Stress: A Guide for All Employers and Employees* (Englewood Cliffs, N.J.: Prentice-Hall, 1980): ix.

People deal differently with the effects of stress. Some have a tolerance for higher levels than others, some are better at reducing the effects of stressors, and some have developed successful coping mechanisms. It is important to recognize what factors produce stress in your life and your job, but it is more important still to develop a good set of coping skills. This is not as complicated as you might think. What are the things that you like to do to relax from a busy schedule or from studying? Do you like to swim, jog, go to the movies, or just get away into the country? List four or five things that you like to do for relaxation.

1.

2.

3.

4.

5.

Keep this list in your mind, and when you feel stressed by job or personal events, find time to pursue one of these activities after work or class or on weekends. Activities like these can help you keep stress under control.

If you could not list four or five relaxing activities, then begin to develop your leisure pursuits. The way in which you use your leisure time can determine how effective you are at work. Hobbies and outside interests are an important part of the coping mechanism. These activities not only renew your interest in your work but can improve your health or prevent stress-related illnesses. Learn to recognize the causes of stress in your life. Try to reduce those stressors where possible and develop your coping skills.

ADDITIONAL RESOURCES

Benson, H. *The Relaxation Response*. New York: Morrow, 1975.

Berlye, Milton K. *Your Career in the World of Work*. Indianapolis: H. W. Sams, 1975.

Bird, C., and T. D. Yutzy. "The Tyranny of Time: Results Achieved versus Hours Spent." *Management Review* (August 1965).

Bliss, Edwin. *Doing It Now*. New York: Scribner's, 1983.

Calano, Jimmy, and Jeff Salzmann. *CareerTracking: 26 Success Shortcuts to the Top*. New York: Simon & Schuster, 1988.

Campbell, David. *If You Don't Know Where You're Going, You'll Probably End Up Somewhere Else*. Allen, Tx.: Argus Communications, 1974.

Greenberg, Herbert M. *Coping with Job Stress: A Guide for All Employers and Employees*. Englewood Cliffs, N.J.: Prentice-Hall, 1980.

Knaus, William. "Why People Procrastinate—Is There a Cure?" *U.S. News and World Report* (October 24, 1983).

Lakein, Alan. *How to Get Control of Your Time and Your Life*. New York: Signet, 1973.

Mackenzie, R. A. *The Time Trap*. New York: American Management Association, 1972.

Miller, Arthur F., Jr. "Discover Your Design." *CPC Annual*. Bethlehem, Pa.: College Placement Council, 1987.

Preziosi, Robert C. "Organization Diagnosis Questionnaire." *The 1980 Annual Handbook for Group Facilitators*. San Diego, Calif.: University Associates, 1980.

Rahe, R. H., and R. D. Arthur. "Holmes-Rahe Adjustment Scale." *Journal of Human Stress* 4 (1978), 3–15.

Scheele, Adele. *Skills for Success: A Guide to the Top for Men and Women*. New York: Ballantine, 1979.

Selye, H. *Stress without Distress,* New York: NAL, 1975.

Yee, M. S., and D. K. Wright. *The Great Escape: A Source Book of Delights and Pleasures for the Mind and Body*. New York: Bantam, 1974.

SECTION 4

Evaluating Your Job Progress

This section focuses on evaluating your progress on the job. Receiving constructive feedback, improving communications between you and your job supervisor, making improvements, developing to your fullest potential, and documenting your experience are the major purposes of the activities in this section.

The first activity is designed to aid you in understanding the nature and purposes of performance evaluation. It explains how performance evaluation systems generally operate and identifies the advantages and disadvantages of your involvement in the process. This activity provides important background information before you actually enter into the performance evaluation process yourself.

Activity 17 takes you through the actual performance evaluation process with your supervisor, using the performance objectives you prepared in an earlier activity. When you have completed this activity, you will know how well you have done on each of your performance objectives, as well as how you have been evaluated on an overall basis.

Getting the most out of the evaluation process is the major goal of Activity 18. In this activity you will identify areas for improvement and then make plans for improving your performance.

The last activity in this section provides guidelines and suggestions for you to follow in preparing a final written report. A copy of this report will be submitted to your college cooperative education/internship coordinator. The report provides you with a portfolio of all the experience you have gained as a result of completing a successful cooperative education/internship experience.

ACTIVITY 16
Understanding the Nature and Purposes of Performance Evaluation

Purpose: To help you understand the nature and purposes of performance evaluation and how this management technique fits into your cooperative education/internship training program.

Everyone who works at a regular job or on a cooperative education/internship assignment is evaluated by his or her job supervisor, whether or not there is a formal evaluation system in place. Evaluations or judgments of an employee's performance are done for a variety of reasons. Documentation of positive feedback, consideration for job promotions, justification for pay raises, authorization for training, and recommendations for new job assignments are all positive reasons for evaluations. Negative reasons include job reassignment, identification of employee weaknesses, disciplinary action against workers, and in some cases dismissal.

Most organizations have a formalized process or system that supervisors use to review and evaluate the job progress of employees. The system is usually referred to as an employee **performance evaluation** system or a performance appraisal or performance review system. Whatever its label, the system is used for many different purposes, including

1. To enhance and improve the communication process between the supervisor and the employee.
2. To improve employee job performance and productivity.
3. To assist the employee in achieving new or expanded job responsibilities and goals.
4. To improve employee–supervisor relationships.
5. To aid the supervisor in helping employees solve work-related problems and concerns.
6. To provide background information required for job and salary adjustments.

A performance evaluation system represents a set of activities directed by management and designed to determine how well employees are carrying out their tasks and job responsibilities. The two types of performance evaluation system most commonly followed by organizations are the **personal traits evaluation method** and the **results evaluation method.**

The majority of performance evaluation systems evaluate employees on the basis of personal traits that are linked to job performance. Traits such as appearance, punctuality, enthusiasm, initiative, dependability, accuracy, follow-through, and creativity are commonly included in the trait performance evaluation method. The method frequently also includes rating the employee on such overall factors as quality and quantity of work performed. Figure 16.1 shows an example of a typical employee evaluation form based primarily on personal traits.

The second type of performance evaluation system is one that permits the supervisor to evaluate employee job performance on the basis of results or preestablished employee performance objectives. Performance objectives such as those you developed in Activity 14 are usually part of an organization's MBO system. Under management by objectives, employees at all levels establish performance objectives with the input of their supervisors in advance of the actual evaluation interview. Then, at evaluation time, employees are evaluated according to how well they have achieved their preestablished performance objectives. Figure 16.2 represents an exam-

Figure 16.1   Example of Personal Traits Performance Evaluation Form

CLEMENT COMMUNITY HOSPITAL EMPLOYMENT EVALUATION

EMPLOYEE _____ DATE _____

JOB TITLE _____ DEPARTMENT _____

Evaluate the employee on the present job position. Circle the number to the left which most nearly expresses your overall judgment on each quality. Also, in the space reserved for comments, consider the employee's performance since the last appraisal and state whether the individual has regressed, remained stationary, or improved in each of the qualities listed. The care and accuracy with which this appraisal is made will determine its value to you, to the employee, and to the organization.

JOB KNOWLEDGE (Consider knowledge of the job gained through experience, general education, specialized training.)
5.   Well informed on all phases of work.
4.   Knowledge thorough enough to perform without assistance.
3.   Adequate grasp of essentials, some assistance required.
2.   Requires considerable assistance.
1.   Inadequate knowledge.
Comments

QUALITY OF WORK (Consider neatness, accuracy and dependability of results regardless of volume.)
5.   Exceptionally accurate, practically no mistakes.
4.   Usually accurate, seldom necessary to check work.
3.   Acceptable, usually neat, occasional errors or rejections.
2.   Often unacceptable, frequent errors or rejections, needs supervision.
1.   Unacceptable, too many errors.
Comments

QUANTITY OF WORK (Consider the volume of work produced under normal conditions. Disregard errors.)
5.   Exceptional quantity, rapid worker, unusually big producer.
4.   Turns out good volume.
3.   Average volume.
2.   Volume below average, often does not complete work.
1.   Very slow worker, cannot complete duties.
Comments

Understanding the Nature and Purposes of Performance Evaluation

Figure 16.1   Example of Personal Traits Performance Evaluation Form (continued)

ABILITY TO LEARN (Consider the speed with which the employee masters new routine and grasps explanations. Consider, also, ability to retain this knowledge.)
5.   Exceptionally fast to learn and adjust to changed conditions, adaptable.
4.   Learns rapidly, follows instructions, retains instructions.
3.   Average instruction required.
2.   Requires extra instructions, necessary to repeat instructions.
1.   Very slow to absorb, poor memory, cannot adapt.
Comments

INITIATIVE (Consider the tendency to contribute, develop and/or carry out new ideas or methods. Also dependability in carrying out routine assignments.)
5.   Excellent, initiative resulting in frequent saving in time and money, always reliable, is a leader.
4.   Very resourceful, can work on own, manages time well, is reliable.
3.   Shows initiative occasionally, usually reliable.
2.   Lacking in initiative, has to be told to complete tasks.
1.   Needs constant prodding, is unreliable.
Comments

COOPERATION AND RELATIONSHIPS (Consider manner of handling job relationships.)
5.   Goes out of way to cooperate with co-workers, supervisors, and subordinates, excellent attitude, takes and gives instruction well.
4.   Gets along well with associates.
3.   Acceptable, usually gets along well, occasionally complains.
2.   Shows reluctance to cooperate, complains.
1.   Very poor cooperation, does not follow instructions, dislikes fellow employees.
Comments

ATTENDANCE (Consider rate of absenteeism, reasons for absenteeism, tardiness, and promptness in giving notice.)
5.   Excellent, absent only for emergencies: family crisis, civic duty, illness; always on time, gives notice when absent.
4.   Rarely absent or late, absent with good reason, gives notice.
3.   Occasionally absent, less important reasons, usually gives notice, but not always in time.
2.   Often absent, lack of adequate notice.
1.   Excessive absenteeism, does not give notice, reasons are unacceptable, cannot be depended upon.
Comments

APPEARANCE (Consider neatness and appropriateness of dress.)
5.   Excellent, always neat and clean.
4.   Good, usually neat and clean.
3.   Average appearance.
2.   Poor, often dirty and careless in appearance.
1.   Unacceptable, offensive.
Comments

OVERALL EVALUATION: Superior _____ Good _____ Satisfactory _____
                                     Unsatisfactory _____

COMMENTS (Consider need for improvement, suitability for job, contributions. BE SPECIFIC!)

CERTIFICATION BY EVALUATOR:
I hereby certify that this appraisal constitutes my best judgment of the service value of this
employee and is based on personal observation and knowledge of the employee's work.

Signature _____   Date _____

CERTIFICATION BY EMPLOYEE:
I hereby certify that I have personally reviewed this report.

Signature _____   Date _____

Approved by _____   Date _____

Source: Theo Haimann and Raymond L. Hilgert, *Supervision: Concepts and Practices of Management* (Cincinnati, OH: South-Western Publishing Company), 1987, pp. 227–228. Reprinted with permission.

Figure 16.2   Cooperative Education/Internship Student Performance Evaluation

Student Name _____   Major _____

Home address _____
          Street   City   State   Zip

Co-op/internship coordinator's name _____

Name of organization _____

Job supervisor's name _____   Work phone (___) _____

Work address _____
          Street   City   State   Zip

Co-op/internship employment dates _____   _____
                                  From   To

STATEMENT OF STUDENT'S PERFORMANCE OBJECTIVES

You will be required to establish five or six performance objectives for each cooperative education/internship period that you complete. These objectives must be originated by you, approved by your job supervisor, and reviewed by your college co-op/internship coordinator. At the end of your cooperative education/internship assignment, you and your job supervisor will rate your progress on each of the performance objectives you have established. The following scale of 1 to 5 is to be used to measure your degree of success in achieving each objective.

* Rating Scale

1 Failed to meet minimum requirements
2 Marginal performance
3 Average or expected performance
4 Better than average performance
5 Outstanding performance

Performance Objectives	*Rating	
	Student	Employer
1.		
2.		

Figure 16.2   Cooperative Education/Internship Student Performance Evaluation (continued)

Performance Objectives	*Rating	
	Student	Employer
3.		
4.		
5.		
6.		

OVERALL EVALUATION: Superior _____ Good _____ Satisfactory _____
Unsatisfactory _____

OTHER COMMENTS:

CERTIFICATION BY JOB SUPERVISOR:
I hereby certify that this rating constitutes my best judgment relative to the performance objectives established by the co-op/internship student for this training assignment period.

Signature _____ Date _____

CERTIFICATION BY CO-OP/INTERNSHIP STUDENT:
I hereby certify that I have personally reviewed this performance evaluation (based on my performance objectives report) with my supervisor.

Signature _____ Date _____

ple of an evaluation system for a cooperative education/internship program in which students are evaluated in terms of preestablished performance objectives. You will use a form similar to this in Activity 17, "Evaluating Your Job Performance." Occasionally, a trait evaluation system and one based on performance objectives are combined into a single performance evaluation system.

As a cooperative education/internship student you should look forward to your performance evaluation. A good evaluation system will provide you with a formal opportunity for two-way communication with your job supervisor. The evaluation process will show you exactly how you are performing on your job. Not only is it a source of positive reinforcement for a job well done but it will also help you identify areas in which you can improve. Obviously, your goals as a cooperative education/internship student is to perform in a satisfactory to above-average manner and to grow on the job. Performance evaluation should not be a frightening or upsetting experience; rather, you should look at the process in terms of its constructive contribution to the success of your assignment.

UNDERSTANDING YOUR ORGANIZATION'S PERFORMANCE EVALUATION SYSTEM

Your organization probably has a performance evaluation system of some type. The system may or may not be complicated and formally defined. A more complex system is not necessarily a better one. It will be to your advantage to find out as much as you can about your organization's performance evaluation system. Performance evaluation can become a valuable tool to help you reach your desired goals during your cooperative education/internship assignment.

Visit the personnel office in your organization and interview someone who is knowledgeable about the performance evaluation system currently in use. After your interview, answer the following questions.

1. Does your organization follow a formal evaluation process or system?

   Yes _____   No _____

   If yes, attach a copy of the forms used for that purpose. If no, explain why no system is currently in place.

2. How frequently are performance evaluations made for employees in your organization?

3. Explain the operation of the performance evaluation system currently in use. Describe the process, including the procedural steps and any required interviews.

BENEFITS OF A PERFORMANCE EVALUATION SYSTEM

You should now be familiar with the performance evaluation system used by your organization. Are cooperative education/internship students evaluated using the same evaluation instrument as regular employees? How can the evaluation system help you in your training program?

Interview your job supervisor to determine what he or she thinks are the major advantages of the present performance evaluation system, to the organization, to you as an employee, and to the supervisor. What are the disadvantages of the performance evaluation system?

Advantages to organization:

Advantages to employees:

Advantages to the supervisor:

Disadvantages of performance evaluation:

USES OF PERFORMANCE EVALUATION INFORMATION

The information collected during the performance evaluation process has many uses in an organization. Ask your job supervisor, as well as one of your co-workers, to explain how the information generated by this process is used. Record their comments in the space provided.

Job supervisor's ideas on uses of information:

Co-worker's ideas on uses of information:

IDENTIFYING AREAS OF JOB PERFORMANCE THAT NEED IMPROVEMENT

One of the major goals of any performance evaluation system is to help people improve their job performance. Develop a list of five or six specific areas in which you think you could improve. Describe them in as much detail as possible and review them with your job supervisor.

REVIEWING YOUR JOB PERFORMANCE OBJECTIVES

Review the performance objectives you developed in Activity 14. In the space provided, explain how the performance objectives you developed can fit into the performance evaluation system used by your organization. Ask your job supervisor to help you with this exercise.

ACTIVITY 17
Evaluating Your Job Performance

Purpose: To help you and your job supervisor complete the evaluation process on the basis of the performance objectives you established in Activity 14.

Each time you complete a cooperative education/internship work assignment period, you will be required to initiate and participate in an evaluation process with your job supervisor. The evaluation is based on the performance objectives you established in Activity 14. Performance objectives, you will recall, are those specific job-related goals or activities you planned to accomplish during your cooperative education/internship training experience. When you developed your performance objectives in Activity 14, you did so with the understanding that those objectives would be a major factor on which your evaluation for the training period would be based. You are now ready to initiate the performance evaluation process, which will permit you to see if you reached your objectives during the work assignment period. The flowchart in Figure 17.1 shows the six steps included in the performance evaluation process.

Organizations that use an MBO system and performance evaluation of employees generally assign the supervisor the responsibility of initiating the evaluation process. Since you are participating in a cooperative education/internship program that requires you to establish performance objectives, you are responsible for initiating the process. Although this approach may appear unnatural to you, in fact it works very well.

GETTING READY FOR THE ACTUAL EVALUATION PROCESS

There are several keys to obtaining the maximum benefit from the performance evaluation process. First and foremost, you should understand that your job supervisor's evaluation of your job performance is not an evaluation of you personally. It is an evaluation of your performance in job-related activities. In other words, you should not take your job supervisor's rating or comments personally. Your job supervisor is not being critical of you as an individual, but rather of what you have done during your cooperative education/internship experience.

Second, it is important to recognize that the performance evaluation process is not designed to create an adversary relationship between you and your job supervisor. Rather, its purpose is to help you improve your job performance through more effective communication with your job supervisor.

The third key to getting the most out of the performance evaluation process is to practice effective listening skills during the interview conference itself. You should make sure that you are hearing the entire message of your job supervisor and hearing it accurately. Before you go through the evaluation interview, review the following strategies that facilitate more effective listening:

1. Communicate to your job supervisor that you are sincerely interested in hearing opinions regarding your progress in your cooperative education/internship assignment.
2. Try to put your job supervisor at ease. Evaluating employee performance is usually not one of a supervisor's favorite responsibilities. You can help your job supervisor feel more comfortable by showing that you are looking forward to the process and that you are genuinely interested in improving.

Figure 17.1

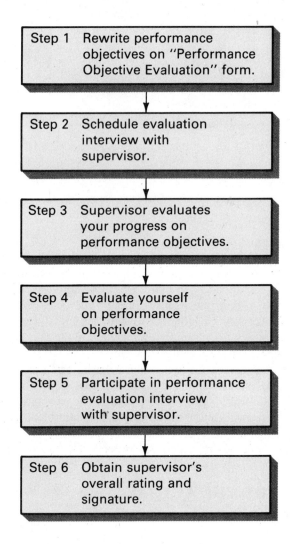

Step 1   Rewrite performance objectives on "Performance Objective Evaluation" form.

Step 2   Schedule evaluation interview with supervisor.

Step 3   Supervisor evaluates your progress on performance objectives.

Step 4   Evaluate yourself on performance objectives.

Step 5   Participate in performance evaluation interview with supervisor.

Step 6   Obtain supervisor's overall rating and signature.

3. When your job supervisor is talking during the interview, listen carefully and try not to interrupt. Simply saying nothing can be helpful in obtaining more information.
4. Don't get angry. Remember, if criticism is offered, it is not directed toward you personally. Arguing with your job supervisor about his or her rating of your job progress will usually not change the rating.
5. Ask questions of your job supervisor during the evaluation conference. This will show that you are really interested in listening to what he or she has to say. For example, you might say, "I understand why you rated me as 'satisfactory.' What could I do to improve my performance in the future?"
6. Restate what you think you are hearing. Restating your job supervisor's points allows you to check on your understanding of the message. It also conveys to your supervisor your sincere interest in what has been said.
7. Avoid distractions. Interruptions can have a serious negative impact on the success of the performance evaluation interview. Try to schedule your performance evaluation conference in a private office or other location where distractions can be minimized.

STEPS IN THE EVALUATION PROCESS

To make the performance evaluation process meaningful and effective, you should follow six steps. Refer to Figure 17.1 to see how these six steps flow together.

Step 1: Rewrite Performance Objectives

Transcribe your finalized and approved performance objectives (prepared in Activity 14, page 127) onto the "Performance Evaluation" form on pages 149 and 150.

Step 2: Schedule Evaluation Conference

Set a date and time with your job supervisor for the purpose of evaluating your job progress on the basis of your performance objectives. Try to schedule the conference at least one week prior to the end of your cooperative education/internship training period. Ask your job supervisor to allow 45 minutes to one hour for this purpose. Explain that the purpose of the evaluation conference is to gain input on your progress during your cooperative education/internship experience by reviewing and evaluating each of your performance objectives. If possible, use a private location where a minimum of interruptions will occur.

Step 3: Ask Job Supervisor for Evaluation

Ask your job supervisor to rate you on each of your performance objectives using the rating scale provided on the "Performance Evaluation" form, page 149.

Step 4: Evaluate Yourself

Review each performance objective carefully and rate (evaluate) yourself on each of your objectives. Use the rating scale provided on the "Performance Evaluation" form on page 149. Do not rate your performance if you have not had an opportunity to work on the objective. As you rate your performance on each objective, don't be too critical of yourself. Likewise, don't overestimate your accomplishments relative to a particular objective. Be honest with yourself.

Step 5: Participate in Evaluation Conference

Keep the appointment you made in Step 2. During the evaluation conference, go over each of your individual performance objectives. Use the "Evaluation Comments" sheet on page 151 if you wish to take notes during the interview.

For each objective, explain why you gave yourself a particular rating. Expand specifically on what you consider to be your strengths and weaknesses. Then ask your job supervisor to share with you the rating he or she gave you on the same objective. Ask your job supervisor to elaborate on the reason for the rating. Request ideas on your strengths and weaknesses with respect to each objective. Ask what you need to do to improve your job performance on each objective. If your rating and your job supervisor's differ, try to find out why.

If you plan to complete another cooperative education/internship experience in the future with the same employer, ask your job supervisor which performance objective should be carried forward into the next training period. Jointly determine, too, what new performance objectives might be included in the next training period. Record these suggestions on the "Evaluation Comments" sheet on page 151.

Step 6: Obtain Job Supervisor's Rating and Signature

Review your job supervisor's overall evaluation of your job progress, note his or her comments, and obtain your job supervisor's signature on the "Performance Evaluation." Then sign the form yourself and return a copy to your college co-op/internship program coordinator. Your signature confirms that you have reviewed all your objectives with your job supervisor and that you understand the reasons for the job supervisor's evaluation of your job progress.

PLANNING FOR IMPROVEMENT

Following the performance evaluation process, you need to specify ways you can improve your job performance. Examine your completed "Performance Evaluation" and "Evaluation Comments'' forms to identify areas in which your performance needs improvement. In the space provided, list these suggestions in the left-hand column. When you return to campus to meet with your co-op/internship coordinator, discuss possible strategies you might follow to improve your performance in each area. Write these strategies in the right-hand column.

Suggested Improvements   Strategies for Improvement

_____

_____

_____

_____

_____

_____

_____

PERFORMANCE EVALUATION

Student name _____ Major _____

Home address _____
                        Street   City   State   Zip

Co-op/internship coordinator's name _____

Name of organization _____

Job supervisor's name _____ Work phone (_____) _____

Work address _____
                        Street   City   State   Zip

Co-op/internship employment dates _____ _____
                                              From   To

STATEMENT OF STUDENT'S PERFORMANCE OBJECTIVES

You will be required to establish five or six performance objectives for each cooperative education/internship period that you complete. These objectives must be originated by you, approved by your job supervisor, and reviewed by your college co-op/internship coordinator. At the end of your cooperative education/internship assignment, you and your job supervisor will rate your progress on each of the performance objectives you have established. The following scale of 1 to 5 is to be used to measure your degree of success in achieving each objective.

* Rating Scale

1 Failed to meet minimum requirements
2 Marginal performance
3 Average performance
4 Better than average performance
5 Outstanding performance

Performance Objectives	*Rating	
	Student	Supervisor
1.		
2.		
3.		

Performance Objectives	*Rating	
	Student	Supervisor
4.		
5.		
6.		

OVERALL EVALUATION: Superior _____ Good _____ Satisfactory _____
Unsatisfactory _____

OTHER COMMENTS:

Certification by job supervisor:
I hereby certify that this rating constitutes my best judgment relative to the performance objectives established by the co-op/internship student for this training assignment period.

Signature _____ Date _____

Certification by co-op/internship student:
I hereby certify that I have personally reviewed this performance evaluation based on my performance objectives report with my supervisor.

Signature _____ Date _____

EVALUATION COMMENTS

ACTIVITY 18
Building on the Evaluation Process

Purpose: To assist you in getting the maximum benefit from the evaluation process carried out in Activity 17.

The purpose of Activity 17 was to lead you through the process of evaluating your performance on the basis of your performance objectives. You should now understand your job supervisor's opinion of your performance with respect to each of these objectives. If this is your final cooperative education/internship assignment period, this process should have given you some valuable information that will be helpful to your career development and progress. If you have further work assignments to complete, you should be able to use the information gathered in the evaluation process to improve your job performance during the next cooperative education/internship training period. For example, perhaps you were unable to fulfill one of your performance objectives because time ran short. You could set that same objective for the next training period. Or perhaps you met an objective only partially because you lacked necessary experience or training. With additional training and experience, you may now be able to accomplish that performance objective fully.

REEXAMINING YOUR EVALUATION

Carefully reread Activity 17, "Evaluating Your Job Performance." Review what happened, what was said, and the notes you took during the process. Also review the general suggestions for improvements that were made at the conclusion of the activity. Then answer the following questions.

1. Identify the performance objectives on which you received a performance rating of "outstanding" or "better than average" from your job supervisor.

    During the evaluation interview, what comments did your job supervisor make regarding those performance objectives?

2. On which performance objectives did you receive an "average" or "marginal" rating from your job supervisor?

   During the evaluation interview, what specific recommendations or suggestions did your job supervisor make to help you improve on those performance objectives?

3. On which performance objectives did you receive a "failed to meet minimum requirements" rating from your job supervisor?

   During the evaluation interview, what specific recommendations or suggestions did your job supervisor make to help you improve on those performance objectives?

4. Your self-rating on each of your performance objectives may have differed from that of your job supervisor. What do you think accounts for those differences? If your rating was higher

than your job supervisor's, what steps can you take to receive a higher rating from your supervisor if this objective is listed for your next performance period?

LOOKING AT IDEAS FOR FUTURE PERFORMANCE OBJECTIVES

Many students using this book will complete several cooperative education/internship experiences as part of their college program. Some students will work for a series of different organizations, but others will continue their employment with the same organization. If you will be continuing your cooperative education/internship experience, please answer the following questions.

1. Which of the performance objectives established in the preceding training period do you think should be continued during the next cooperative education/internship assignment?

2. During your evaluation interview, did your job supervisor make any suggestions that could be included in your performance objectives for the next training period?

You should now have a clear understanding of performance evaluation. Use this knowledge to improve on your weaknesses and build on your strengths for future assignments. Please answer the following questions to sum up the process.

1. At the bottom of the evaluation form, your job supervisor was required to give you an overall rating for your job performance during the cooperative education/internship training period.

   What was the overall rating given by your job supervisor?

   Superior _____ Good _____ Satisfactory _____ Unsatisfactory _____

If you were rated in either the "good," "satisfactory," or "unsatisfactory" category, what do you think you need to do to improve your overall rating? What suggestions or ideas for overall improvement did your job supervisor make during the evaluation interview?

2. List the strengths and weaknesses of your job performance that you were able to identify as a result of establishing performance objectives, completing your cooperative education/internship work assignment, and going through the evaluation process.

    Strengths that you identified:

    a.

    b.

    c.

    Weaknesses that you identified:

    a.

    b.

    c.

    What will you do to address and correct the weaknesses?

3. What is your overall opinion concerning the performance evaluation process?

ACTIVITY 19
Writing a Final Work Report

Purpose: To provide you with instructions and format for preparation of your final written cooperative education/internship report.

At the conclusion of each work assignment or series of assignments, you will be expected to write a final report. The written report is commonly referred to as a "work report" or "student report." If prepared at the end of a series of cooperative education/internship work assignments, it is sometimes labeled "final work report" or "senior report." From college to college, work reports will vary in complexity, length, and items to be included. Figure 19.1 shows what is required in the final senior report at a typical four-year college. Figure 19.2 shows the requirements for a two-year college.

Does your college require a written work report at the conclusion of the cooperative education/internship assignment period?

Yes _____   No _____

If yes, what are the major section titles for the content of the report?

1.

2.

3.

4.

5.

6.

7.

The purpose of the written work report is to summarize what you have learned as a result of your cooperative education/internship experience. Not only is this written work report helpful to you but it is also useful for future co-op/internship students who may choose to work for that same employing organization.

GUIDELINES FOR PREPARATION OF A WRITTEN WORK REPORT

Before you prepare your written work report, you should review the following format guidelines, which will help to ensure that you write a high-quality report:

1. The report should be typewritten, double-spaced, on standard 8½"-by-11" paper.
2. The report should have an appropriate cover page showing the following information:
   a. Your name
   b. Name of your employing organization
   c. Your cooperative education/internship position title
   d. Dates employed

Figure 19.1   Senior Report Requirements for a Four-Year College

Senior Report
Virginia Polytechnic and State University
Blacksburg, Virginia

Senior Report. A written report on the total Co-op Program is required of all seniors. The Co-op may choose his/her own format; the only requirement is that the report be logical and informative. It should be typed (on 8½" × 11" paper) and submitted no later than the end of the fall quarter of the senior year.

The Co-op may choose his/her own points for discussion, but the following topics should be covered, as a minimum:

Work Experience—Summarize the total experience that you gained on the job as the work quarters were completed.

Relevancy to Total Education—Comment on the degree to which your job experience added to your education in your major field and to your total education and preparation for employment after graduation.

Life in the Employer's Environment—Comment on your working associations. Did your responsibilities increase with time? Were you accepted by your co-workers? Helped by them and your supervisor? Did you feel that you were a contributing member of your organization? Was the job satisfying (on a quarter-by-quarter and overall basis)? Did you feel that your employer was interested in your future?

Living Arrangements—If you lived away from home, comment on the availability of lodging and on expenses; also describe cultural and social opportunities.

Financial Considerations—Briefly outline how your Co-op salary benefited you and was utilized during your college career.

General Critique—What is your overall opinion of Co-op as an alternative to the regular college program? What *constructive* recommendations would you offer to improve the policies and operation of our program?

SOURCE: Cooperative Education Department, Virginia Polytechnic and State University, Blacksburg, Virginia. Reprinted with permission.

Figure 19.2　Final Report Requirements for a Two-Year College

Final Review and Evaluation
Student Self-Evaluation
Utah Valley Community College

On the basis of each of the objectives and related assignments you determined at the start of the quarter, please tell how you feel you have reached and satisfied the requirements of the course. Be as specific as possible, detailing what you have accomplished for each objective.

1. **Career Orientation** (Identify what you did to see the different aspects of your career area, or something else you accomplished in the career growth area.)

2. **Skills Acquisition Objective** (Identify a specific skill or bit of knowledge that you were able to acquire during the quarter.)

3. **Skills Application Objective** (Identify some skill or bit of knowledge that you were able to improve upon, or where you became more proficient.)

4. **Human Relations Objective** (Identify one way you improved your ability to work with supervisors, fellow workers, or others with whom you were associated.)

5. **Additional Objective** (Identify what you were able to do in terms of completing an additional objective in your job assignment.)

6. **Related Assignments** (Identify any additional job-related assignments you completed during your cooperative education/internship experience.)

SOURCE: Carl Johnson, Utah Valley Community College, Orem, Utah. Reprinted with permission.

3. The report should be written in language that is easily understandable to a reader who is unfamiliar with the cooperative education/internship program and your assignment.
4. Use appropriate words and correct sentence structure, spelling, and paragraphing. Careless writing may have a negative impact on the overall evaluation of your final written report.
5. The use of drawings, pictures, graphs, charts, descriptions, and materials to supplement the written part of your report is strongly encouraged.
6. A bibliography of individuals and publications consulted during the preparation of the report should be included.

PREPARING A WRITTEN WORK REPORT

The preparation of a written work report should not be a difficult assignment for you. During the process, refer to the completed activities in this book. For example, when you constructed or revised your job description in Activity 13, prepared performance objectives in Activity 14, and underwent the performance evaluation process outlined in Activity 17, you fulfilled some of the requirements of the written report.

As you prepare your written report, you may wish to consider including the following items. If your college specifies its own content and format for a written report, be sure that you follow its suggestions and requirements. You should submit a copy of your finished report to your college co-op/internship coordinator. Providing a copy to your employing organization is optional.

1. Discuss each of your performance objectives using the following outline (attach any supporting information you wish):
   a. List each performance objective and explain why you selected it.
   b. Tell how you originally planned to fulfill the objective.
   c. Tell what aspects of the plan worked.
   d. How did you change your original plan?
   e. Report on how effectively you met your objectives.
   f. How useful were the performance objectives to your own skill development? Consider the full range of human skills: manual and technical, communications (speaking, listening, reading, and writing), and human relations.
   g. How useful were the selected performance objectives to your employer?
   h. If you were not able to begin or accomplish a performance objective, please state the reason.
2. Briefly list your major responsibilities and the duties that you performed during your cooperative education/internship assignment.
3. Evaluate or explain in detail the relevancy of your cooperative education/internship assignment to your current career objectives. Describe the relationships you see between your college major and your cooperative education/internship experience.
4. Identify any strengths or weaknesses you have discovered in yourself as a result of your cooperative education/internship experience.
5. Identify any noteworthy job-related accomplishments or achievements that are the result of your cooperative education/internship experience.
6. What do you consider to be the best or strongest features of your cooperative education/internship assignment? What do you consider to be the less desirable features of your cooperative education/internship assignment?
7. Explain how your cooperative education/internship experience has affected your attitudes toward yourself, toward others, and toward your future educational plans.
8. What recommendations would you make to the organization where you have been working relative to employing co-op/internship students in the future?
9. What recommendations would you make to your college regarding using this organization as a future employer of co-op/internship students?
10. What specific suggestions or recommendations would you make to a future co-op/internship student in regard to working for this same employer?
11. What impact do you think your cooperative education/internship experience will have on your future career plans and development?

12. Co-op/internship students usually have no difficulty identifying job skills that they have developed or refined as a result of their work experience. Identifying learning that is not specific to the job, however, is somewhat more difficult. Explain some of the other things you have learned about people, work, and organizations as a result of your cooperative education/internship experience.
13. Explain how your cooperative education/internship experience improved your ability to work with others, including your supervisor and your fellow workers.
14. Identify a problem area in the organization where you completed your work assignment.
    a. Define the problem clearly.
    b. Outline all the relevant information surrounding the problem.
    c. Provide suggestions for alternatives that would address this problem.
    d. State your best solution, explaining the rationale for your choice.
15. On the basis of your observations in your present job environment, how would you characterize the general attitude of the employees toward work? Do you believe this represents the typical view of the work ethic in our current society?

EVALUATING YOUR COOPERATIVE EDUCATION/INTERNSHIP EXPERIENCE

Many cooperative education/internship programs ask their students to evaluate their experience at the conclusion of the work assignment. The purpose of such an evaluation is to provide information to the college prior to placing other students with the same employing organization. Please complete the "Confidential Student Evaluation of the Cooperative Education/Internship Work Experience" form on pages 161 and 162. Attach the completed form to your final written report and turn it in to your college cooperative education/internship office.

CONFIDENTIAL STUDENT EVALUATION OF
THE COOPERATIVE EDUCATION/INTERNSHIP
WORK EXPERIENCE

Student name: _____ Major: _____

Employer (name of organization) _____

Location _____

Job supervisor's name _____

Description of duties: _____

_____

Please rate your work experience during this past work period according to the following criteria. Make additional comments if you wish. The purpose of the form is to provide opportunity for frank appraisal of the job location in the interests of the employer and future students. Please place a check mark beside your rating.

Work experience relates to field of study

High _____ Good _____ Average _____ Poor _____ Very poor _____ No observation _____

Adequacy of employer supervision

High _____ Good _____ Average _____ Poor _____ Very poor _____ No observation _____

Helpfulness of job supervisor

High _____ Good _____ Average _____ Poor _____ Very poor _____ No observation _____

Cooperativeness of fellow workers

High _____ Good _____ Average _____ Poor _____ Very poor _____ No observation _____

Opportunity to use academic training

High _____ Good _____ Average _____ Poor _____ Very poor _____ No observation _____

Opportunity to develop human relations skills

High _____ Good _____ Average _____ Poor _____ Very poor _____ No observation _____

Provision for levels of responsibility consistent with student ability and growth

High _____ Good _____ Average _____ Poor _____ Very poor _____ No observation _____

Opportunity to develop communication skills

High _____ Good _____ Average _____ Poor _____ Very poor _____ No observation _____

Opportunity to develop creativity skills

High _____ Good _____ Average _____ Poor _____ Very poor _____ No observation _____

Opportunity to solve problems

High _____ Good _____ Average _____ Poor _____ Very poor _____ No observation _____

Opportunity to develop critical thinking skills

High _____ Good _____ Average _____ Poor _____ Very poor _____ No observation _____

Helpfulness of faculty coordinator

High _____ Good _____ Average _____ Poor _____ Very poor _____ No observation _____

Helpfulness of university (cooperative education/internship) office

High _____ Good _____ Average _____ Poor _____ Very poor _____ No observation _____

Did the assignment meet _____ exceed _____ or fall below _____ your expectations?

Would you want to work for this organization again? Yes _____ No _____

Would you please give your employer an overall evaluation?

Excellent _____ Very good _____ Good _____ Average _____

Would you recommend the cooperative education/internship program to other students in your field? Yes _____ No _____

Please make specific comments to help us in further evaluating your cooperative education/internship experience. _____

_____

_____   _____
(Student signature)   (Date)

ADDITIONAL RESOURCES

Chapman, Elwood N. *Supervisor's Survival Kit*. 4th ed. Chicago: Science Research Associates, 1985.

Megginson, Leon C., Donald C. Mosley, and Paul H. Pietri. *Supervisory Management*. Cincinnati: South-Western Publishing Co., 1985.

Plunkett, Richard W. *Supervision: The Direction of People at Work*. 3rd ed. Dubuque, Iowa: William C. Brown, 1983.

Williams, J. Clifton, Andrew J. DuBrin, and Henry L. Sisk. *Management and Organization*. Cincinnati: South-Western Publishing Co., 1985.

SECTION 5

Building for the Future

The activities in the final section of this book are designed to help you use the concepts presented earlier as building blocks for future success. Activity 20 focuses on making that critical transition from your cooperative education/internship assignment to your first job after graduation. Activity 21 addresses the important topic of promotions.

Because we all must make changes at various times in our lives, including job changes, the next four activities deal with change and how you might prepare for it. Understanding change and the reasons for it, preparing yourself with additional education and training, and developing your network of contacts are activities designed to make coping with change less burdensome.

Taking a look at your previous experiences, your successes, and your accomplishments and putting them together in a package that is attractive to future employers are the purposes of Activity 26, ''Developing Your Personal Marketing Plan.'' This plan should be useful to you both now and at any other time that you feel the need to seek a new position.

A cooperative education/internship guide would not be complete without allowing you and assisting you to evaluate your total program. Was the cooperative education/internship program beneficial to you? Helping you to answer that question is the purpose of the final activity.

You have accomplished a great deal—from planning for the experience in Section 1 through preparing for it and developing your training program in Sections 2 and 3, to evaluating your job progress in Section 4. Now you must use this knowledge and experience to build for the future. Completing the eight activities in Section 5 will allow you to maximize the benefits of your experience. It's your career. Go for it!

ACTIVITY 20
Making the Transition to Permanent Employment

---

*Purpose: To assist you in making the transition from your cooper-
ative education/internship experience to your first position following graduation.*

Finding the job they want and being happy in their work are goals that most people set for
themselves. Counselors and teachers involved in career development, career counseling, and
cooperative education have been working with students for years to provide guidance and placement assistance designed to improve satisfaction with jobs and career choices. Many studies, such
as those conducted by the College Placement Council (CPC) and its member institutions, have
indicated a high degree of job satisfaction among graduates. In *Job Satisfaction after College: The
College Graduates' Viewpoint,* the CPC Foundation reported that only 4 percent of their sample of
4138 respondents selected "not at all" when asked "How satisfied are you with your current
job?" and given the choices "very satisfied," "somewhat satisfied," and "not at all satisfied."[1]

The CPC Foundation survey, however, made it clear that, although satisfaction appears high,
"too little is known about job satisfaction." In pursuing the question and trying to define "a good
job," the CPC identified several factors that influence job satisfaction. Among the most important
ones are possessing a drive to achieve, holding policy-making responsibility, designing one's own
work program, having a job at the professional level, receiving a high salary, and fully utilizing
skills. Significant is this statement: "Of all possible influences on job satisfaction examined here,
by far the most potent are characteristics of the current job. One can easily predict a given
individual's level of job satisfaction by knowing the circumstances of his or her work situation."[2]
It is important, therefore, that the matter of moving from your cooperative education/internship
program to permanent employment be given considerable attention.

PLANNING FOR YOUR FIRST JOB
AFTER GRADUATION

In an excellent article for the *CPC Annual,* Keith Johnson points out: "What you do (and are
allowed to do) in your first position will help determine your future potential." He suggests that
you "consider both immediate and longer-range factors" before making your choice.[3]

Look back at Activity 1. What were some of your important personal and work values? If you
emphasized such things as salary, type of work, desire for friendly work environment, and strong
benefit package, you are concerned primarily with immediate factors. If, on the other hand, your
choices favored such considerations as opportunity for personal growth, chance for continuing
education, opportunities for promotion, and movement into management, you are looking at
longer-range factors. It is these longer-range factors that lead to job satisfaction over time.

---

[1] College Placement Council, *Job Satisfaction after College: The College Graduates' Viewpoint* (Bethlehem, Pa.: CPC
Foundation, 1977): 6.
[2] Ibid., p. 24.
[3] Keith Johnson, "Your First Position: Springboard or Hurdle?" *CPC Annual* (Bethlehem, Pa.: College Placement
Council, 1987): 46.

When you completed the work values clarification exercise in Activity 1, you compared a short list of work values. Here is a longer list of 32 work values, from "Finding the Job That Fits," by Dillion and White.[4] Place a check in the appropriate column beside each value to indicate whether it is very important to you or less important.

Values That May Be Important When Selecting a Job

	Very Important	Less Important
Amount and timing of travel	_____	_____
Amount of possible overtime	_____	_____
Benefits	_____	_____
Compensation	_____	_____
Congenial work colleagues	_____	_____
Dynamic executive or top management personnel	_____	_____
Employer work policies	_____	_____
Evaluation process (how and when I am evaluated)	_____	_____
Geographic mobility (whether I can be transferred to other locations)	_____	_____
Job security	_____	_____
Location	_____	_____
Opportunity of challenging work situations	_____	_____
Opportunity for continued formal education	_____	_____
Opportunity for continued informal education	_____	_____
Opportunity to move into other segments of the company	_____	_____
Parking facilities	_____	_____
Physical location of job site	_____	_____
Potential for added responsibility	_____	_____
Potential for advancement (promotion)	_____	_____
Potential for independent work	_____	_____
Potential for varied work experience	_____	_____
Potential growth of company	_____	_____
Prestige of the business or organization	_____	_____
Professional environment of the workplace	_____	_____
Rewards tied to performance, not seniority	_____	_____
Routine vs. nonroutine work	_____	_____
Significance of the job to the company (potential to contribute)	_____	_____

---

[4] R. D. Dillion and P. E. White, "Finding the Job That Fits," *Journal of Career Planning and Employment* 48, no. 3 (March 1988): 62.

	Very Important	Less Important
Social status of the job	_____	_____
Stability of the company	_____	_____
Use of talents on the job	_____	_____
Work environment	_____	_____
Work hours (flexible or inflexible)	_____	_____

Notice which kinds of values you rated very important and which are less important. Shortly you can use this list to determine which values are related to short-term and long-range goals.

MOTIVATION ON THE JOB

Frederick Herzberg has written extensively about work and motivation. There are some factors, he says, that rarely motivate workers; he calls them **hygiene factors.** These factors are important *only* when absent. In other words, the absence of these factors produce dissatisfaction. Factors such as salary, benefits, working conditions, and supervision are hygiene factors.

According to Herzberg's formulation, those factors that are related to personal growth and development are the ones that motivate employees. Factors such as the nature of the work itself, opportunity for advancement, chance to achieve, and personal recognition are **motivation factors.**

The same list of 32 factors that you just rated is repeated here, with an *H* (hygiene factor) or an *M* (motivation factor) next to each value. Place the appropriate letter (*M* or *H*) beside each check mark on the values chart that you just completed.

Values That May Be Important When Selecting a Job

M	Amount and timing of travel
H	Amount of possible overtime
H	Benefits
H	Compensation
H	Congenial work colleagues
M	Dynamic executive or top management personnel
M	Employer work policies
M	Evaluation process (how and when I am evaluated)
H	Geographic mobility (whether I can be transferred to other locations)
H	Job security
H	Location
M	Opportunity of challenging work situations
M	Opportunity for continued formal education
M	Opportunity for continued informal education
M	Opportunity to move into other segments of the company
H	Parking facilities
H	Physical location of job site
M	Potential for added responsibility
M	Potential for advancement (promotion)
M	Potential for independent work
M	Potential for varied work experience
M	Potential growth of company
M	Prestige of the business or organization
M	Professional environment of the workplace
M	Rewards tied to performance, not seniority
H	Routine vs. nonroutine work
M	Significance of the job to the company (potential to contribute)
M	Social status of the job
H	Stability of the company

M	Use of talents on the job
H	Work environment
H	Work hours (flexible or inflexible)

Compare the two columns of your list. If you have more *M*s in your "very important" list, you should look for a position with longer-range possibilities. If your "very important" list contains more *H*s, the hygiene factors are more important to you right now. Realize, however, that as you fulfill those needs your level of satisfaction may not rise appreciably. Pursuit of short-range goals could lead you to some dead-end jobs. It is up to you to decide what is important to you right now. Is it short-range, immediate gratification of needs or some longer-range, future possibilities that will provide satisfaction for you?

WHAT CAN YOU OFFER AN EMPLOYER?

At the same time as you are evaluating each potential employer, these employers are evaluating you. What is it about the cooperative education/internship experience that interests employers? Three notable studies of perceived employer benefits were conducted during the 1970s, the first by Arthur D. Little Research Corporation, the second by the Detroit Institute of Technology, and the third by Applied Management Sciences. In all three studies, employers were asked to identify (and in some cases to quantify) the specific benefits they associated with employing cooperative education/internship students.

In all the studies, employers cited the quality of the work performed by students, the favorable cost/benefit ratio, the ability to identify and recruit prospective permanent employees, the ability to recruit graduates with more highly developed skills, and the productivity of these skilled workers immediately upon employment, with little or no training. As an additional benefit, employers noted that retention rates of these graduates were better, that promotions occurred sooner and more frequently, and that these graduates moved into management positions earlier than graduates without such experiences. Therefore, it should be of interest to you to examine the list of benefits provided in Figure 20.1 and be sure to emphasize salient ones that apply to you when interviewing for the position you want.

COMMON BUSINESS PROCEDURES

Once you begin your first permanent job, a knowledge of standard business practices will be important to you. You may have been exposed to only a few as a cooperative education/internship student. How well and how quickly you develop common business skills is critical, regardless of your major or your assignment.

Greeting People

If you have not become skilled in greeting people (clients, co-workers, supervisors, subordinates), you must learn to do so from the moment you begin the job. You need to know how to meet people, to address them professionally, to be introduced and to introduce clients or co-workers to others, and to use calling cards effectively. Even though American business standards today are much less formal than in earlier times, not all aspects of protocol have been discontinued. In fact, much of the skill required in meeting and greeting people is embedded in common rules of politeness and courtesy. These rules apply whether the greeting is in person, on the telephone, or in written form. Develop a courteous attitude and treat people with respect. The old proverb "Do unto others as you would have them do unto you" is not a bad watchword to follow.

Using the Telephone

Even though customers, clients, bosses, and co-workers usually cannot see you through the telephone, you should respond as if they could. Be attentive, reassuring, interested, and friendly. The telephone can be a great friend or a despised enemy. Spend only the time necessary to

Figure 20.1

Recruitment Yields

Recruitment yield in terms of persons hired, as a percent of candidates interviewed, was 13 times higher for co-op students (40%) than for recent college graduates (3%).

EEO Objectives

The percentage of minority group members hired was twice as high among co-op students (33%) as among recent college graduates (16%), for the four-year period ended June 30, 1974.

Work Performance

Employer ratings of work performance, based on a scale of 4.00 for excellent, averaged 2.82 for co-op students, 3.03 for co-op graduates, and 2.89 for other recent college graduates in the ten-year period ended June 30, 1974.

Employee Retention

The employment of half of the co-op students terminated before college graduation, but 62% of co-op graduates received regular job offers and 79% of offers were accepted. After graduation, the termination rate of co-op graduates (18%) was less than among other college graduates (22%).

Salary and Promotional Progression

Co-op graduates received merit raises in salary more frequently than other college graduates. Co-op graduates received an average of one promotion every two years—compared to once every three years for other college graduates. Co-op graduates received more promotions to supervisory positions, and they received them sooner, than other college graduates.

Supplemental Costs and Benefits

Employers reported more flexibility in assigning work to co-op students than to college graduates, differing experience concerning the effect of co-op students on the time of other staff members, better relationships with colleges, difficulties in scheduling work periods, and variations in administrative costs.

Recruitment Costs

Recruitment costs averaged much less for co-op students ($50) than for recent college graduates ($800). Among individual employers, recruitment cost per co-op student ranged from 5% to 70% of the cost of recruiting a recent college graduate. None of the employers reported higher recruitment costs for the co-op.

Labor Costs

Co-op students received lower salaries and fewer employee benefits than recent college graduates. Total labor costs averaged 40% less for co-op students than for recent college graduates. Starting salaries of co-op graduates were 9% higher than for other college graduates.

NOTE: This Summary appeared in "Employer Experience with Cooperative Education: Analysis of Costs and Benefits," Detroit, MI: The Detroit Institute of Technology, 1976, a research study under Title IVD of the Higher Education Act of 1965, by Richard A. Hayes and Jill H. Travis.

establish rapport and to transact your business. Business calls normally should not be prolonged or rambling. Before terminating the call, be sure to say "thank you," regardless of the call's originator or purpose.

Before placing a call, be sure to plan what you wish to say. Organize your presentation logically and succinctly. Keep its purpose clearly in mind and don't stray too far afield. Ask questions to test clarity and understanding. Use language that is direct and unambiguous. Keep paper and pencil handy and make notes as appropriate. Have materials ready and don't fumble about, keeping the other party waiting while you look for them.

If you must answer the telephone for others, have message slips available. Take down the information completely, asking the caller to repeat if necessary. Be sure of the spelling of the caller's name and organization and double-check the telephone number. If you need to place a caller on hold or transfer a call, please let the caller know what you are doing and what he or she should expect. Give the caller the opportunity to decide whether he or she wants that option. When transferring a call, be sure the caller has the new number and name in case the call disconnects.

Above all, learn how to use your company's telephone system and its features. Today, you have the possibility of holding calls, forwarding, intercepting, transferring, conferencing, redialing automatically, and numerous other options. Know how to perform those functions that will assist you in making more effective and efficient use of your telephone time, including the use of direct distance dialing, telephone credit cards, and WATS lines. Be aware of time zones and the difference in time between you and the person you are calling.

Making Travel Plans

If you will be traveling on business, first familiarize yourself with the travel policies and procedures of your organization and its requirements for documentation of expenses. Obtain copies of travel guidelines, if available, and any forms required. Find out if your organization uses a specific travel agency. If the organization does any volume of business with airlines and hotels, a travel agency probably has been selected and can provide convenient, consistent, and discounted service for all employees traveling on business. Chances are the travel agent is aware of the organization's requirements regarding level and class of service.

Whether you use an agency or make your own arrangements, it is important that you plan your itinerary before you do anything else. You must know where you are going, when, and what your approximate schedule will be, plus any other restrictions or limitations. For example, you should not plan to fly out in the early morning for a late morning meeting (unless using a shuttle flight) because delays could cause you to miss the meeting. Know whether you need to arrive the evening before a meeting and what problems a delay could cause. When you call to make your reservations, have your itinerary in front of you so that you can understand the effect of alternative arrangements.

When scheduling flights and hotel rooms, know your organization's requirements. Some companies specify only coach seating on airlines; some permit first class. There may be limitations on how much you can spend for a hotel room or a preference for certain hotel chains. Some organizations have special arrangements with hotel chains for their employees. These arrangements not only apply to level of service but may provide for direct billing as well. You might need to arrange in advance for use of the organization's credit cards.

Having an itinerary also helps you to plan your wardrobe for packing, both for each scheduled event and for your own comfort. You can see when you need less formal clothing (travel, off hours, informal seminars) and when you require appropriate business attire (formal meetings, client gatherings, important dinner meetings). Your wardrobe will determine the size and type of luggage needed. Perhaps an overnight bag and briefcase are enough for a short trip, whereas a longer trip might require a large suitcase, a small carry-on, and a briefcase. For longer trips, try to pack essentials—important papers, a change of clothing—in carry-on luggage. Then lost or delayed checked baggage will not cause significant problems.

Determine company policies regarding use of taxis, airport limousines, and rental cars. You would not want to use a rental car and then discover that the expense is not reimbursable. This kind of lesson can be costly. The same applies to meals while traveling. Know the policies on reimbursement for your own meals and those of your clients, as well as any limits or restrictions that apply.

Foreign business travel requires a more complicated set of procedures. Arrangements must be made far in advance for passports, visas, and immunizations. Although foreign airline reservations may not be significantly more complicated than in the United States, hotel reservations and currency exchanges pose special problems that may require the assistance of a travel agent. Be sure you know what documents will be necessary and become familiar with any special conditions or restrictions. On either domestic or foreign travel, plan your needs for cash and/or traveler's checks in advance. Leave a margin for error in estimating needs.

Using Expense Reports

Before traveling, check your organization's policies and procedures regarding mileage rates (for your automobile), other transportation, tolls, parking, meals, tipping, and conference registration fees. Review the necessary expense forms and be sure you know when receipts will be required. Failure to produce such receipts could be cause for nonreimbursement and perhaps future tax problems. Above all, keep careful and detailed records of your travel expenses. If your organization uses a per diem system for expenses, or has special provisions regarding travel advances, be sure you understand how they work.

Using Credit Cards

For ease of travel, whether on business or pleasure, consider the use of credit cards. Determine which credit cards allow you the flexibility you need, coupled with acceptability and convenience. Since rates of interest and annual fees, service charges, billing cycles, and credit requirements vary, compare credit card companies for compatibility with your budget. Determine the terms and conditions and the background information you will need to provide on the application.

Do you possess any credit cards now? Make a list of those you have currently. In the column labeled "Limits," list the dollar limit for each card, and in the column labeled "Uses," list those travel uses that are allowed (for example, hotels, airline tickets, ready cash). If you have no credit cards or none that would be useful in travel, such as retail store credit cards or local bank cards, list those that you feel would be worth obtaining.

Credit Card	Limits	Uses
_____	_____	_____
_____	_____	_____
_____	_____	_____
_____	_____	_____
_____	_____	_____

SHORT- AND LONG-RANGE GOALS

In making the transition to permanent employment, it is in your best interest to consider some of your short- and long-range goals. After all, job satisfaction is directly linked to how well, or how poorly, your position allows you to satisfy your goals. In the space provided, list some of the goals that you have set for yourself. These can be personal goals, career goals, leisure goals, or lifetime goals. (Don't spend more than five minutes making your list.)

To the left of each goal, make a notation of *S* for immediate or short-range goals (less than three years) or *L* for longer-range ones.

When assessing your selection of permanent employment, ask yourself which of your short-range goals this choice will enable you to accomplish. The answer will determine how well the organization will serve your immediate needs. Then ask yourself how many of your longer-range goals are likely to be fulfilled. The answer will determine how well you will be satisfied, over time, working for the organization.

Look at your list of goals again. Are they specific or vague? Try to be as specific as possible. Is each one both achievable and appropriate for you? Nothing is more frustrating than pursuing unrealistic goals. Will these goals allow you to stretch yourself? Goals that are easily attainable might not present enough challenge. Do these goals reflect your personal and work values? Your goals must be a reflection of your own personal value set. Do these goals include a variety of tasks? Goals that are too narrow don't allow for breadth of talents and skills. Compare your list with the values you identified in Activity 1.

David Campbell wrote a book on career development entitled *If You Don't Know Where You're Going, You'll Probably End Up Somewhere Else*. Without goals, who knows where you might end up? More important, though, you may not experience a great deal of satisfaction on the job or in your career and may feel the need to change jobs too frequently. Each job change can be costly, in terms of both money and effort. A change should be made to improve your career, not just alter it.

ACTIVITY 21
Maximizing Your Promotional Opportunities

Purpose: To point out the difference between college and the world of permanent employment and to assist you in adopting behavior designed to advance your career.

A recently sighted bumper sticker stated, "Winners have learned to do things that losers do not want to do." Humor aside, this statement offers an important message to those who wish to succeed and move ahead on the job. You cannot expect a promotion until you have demonstrated that you can do the job you have better than anyone else. Yet knowing that you are doing a good job and having it recognized as such are two different matters.

In college, you probably made few decisions that affected anyone other than yourself. Your work was always graded so that you received feedback in a relatively short period of time, and others besides yourself were concerned with your career development. In the real world of work, as you probably have noticed from your cooperative education/internship assignments, you may receive little feedback, very infrequently, and very few positive reinforcements. No one seems to care about your career except you. Evaluation might occur once a year, if that often. So how will you know if you are doing a good job? In his book *Moving Up,* Eli Djeddah says, "The signs of how you are doing on a job are easy to read. When you are on your way up, your duties are broadened, your title is changed, and you are rewarded financially. When you are on the way out, your duties are narrowed, your life is diminished, and your pay is reduced."[1]

The purpose of this activity is to help you continue to grow on the job and take positive steps to promote yourself and enhance your career.

LEARN THE NORMS OF THE ORGANIZATION

Do you know what norms are? When you enter a new situation or a new group, do you feel uncomfortable? This response results from not knowing what to expect or what will be expected of you. **Norms** are the unwritten rules of relationships and behaviors that operate in any organization or group of people. Each person in an organization learns, often unconsciously, to recognize the norms, although they are never codified. A violation of the norms can result in loss of a sense of belonging and even in ostracism.

But how does someone who is new to the group learn what the norms are? Norms are learned by observation. Think about experiences you have had in joining new groups on campus or beginning a new course with different classmates. When you first entered that group, what did you notice about the group's behavior? Did class start at the signal of the bell or when the instructor sensed that everyone was there? Did students speak up spontaneously or raise their hands and wait to be recognized? Did you ever have the experience of sitting in someone else's favorite seat? Each of these behaviors represented the operation of a norm. When you sat in someone else's favorite seat, the discomfort resulted from the fact that you were breaking an unwritten code, a norm.

---

[1] Eli Djeddah, *Moving Up: How to Get High Salaried Jobs* (Berkeley, Calif.: Ten Speed Press, 1971): 121.

In the space provided, list some of the norms that you observed operating in the organization where you worked on your cooperative education/internship assignment.

How did you learn to recognize those norms?

Were any of the norms different from guidelines written in the organization's policy manuals?

It is not uncommon for norms to be in direct conflict with stated policies. In order to become part of the group, you must learn to identify appropriate norms and adhere to them when they are not in conflict with management expectations. When norms are inappropriate (such as coming in whenever you wish—even though the boss expects you to be prompt), you need to reject them. It would be easy for you to fall into the trap of thinking, "Everyone is doing it, therefore it must be all right." Your personal standards and your integrity require that you behave properly, regardless of the norms that have developed. As Shakespeare said in *Hamlet:*

> This above all: to thine own self be true,
> And it must follow, as the night the day,
> Thou canst not then be false to any man.

During this initial period of observation and learning, get to know your organization and the unit in which you work. What is the mission of the organization? What are the goods or services that it produces? What is the specific purpose of the unit in which you work? How is the organization structured? Read organizational literature and talk with people, particularly senior personnel. What do the company officers value? You can't begin to understand what you must do to be successful unless you know what is important to the organization and its key players.

In recent years, the term **corporate culture** has been applied to the practices, beliefs, and values of an organization. This is not a bad analogy. Like ethnic groups, organizations develop a set of norms, rules, and procedures—ways of behaving—that employees must learn if they want to move forward and to be rewarded. In an article called "Understanding Corporate Culture," Gary Cluff says, "Increasingly, the focus is on values and ethics as the keys to corporate greatness."[2] He cites those values he considers important: employee attitudes, work atmosphere, internal communications, management style, employment opportunity, stability, business ethics, corporate purpose, and consumer relations. The questions he suggests that you ask yourself in each of these areas are very enlightening. Here is a sample of them:

- How do employees feel about the organization? Do they speak of the company with pride, or do they guard what they say for fear of reprisals?
- Is the atmosphere warm and friendly, or cold and distant?
- Can employees articulate the goals of the company, or do they seem unsure? Do they know what is expected of them?
- How are decisions made? Are they made only by top management or is there a shared decision-making style?
- Does the company promote from within, or do they prefer to go outside? Do they have management training programs and are they accessible to all? What is the company's turnover rate and how does that compare industry-wide?
- Is the organization "old" and traditional in its approach, or is innovation appreciated?
- Is the emphasis heavily on the profit-at-any-cost motive, or does the company seem concerned about the needs of its employees and society at large?
- How does the corporation and its management see its image in the community? Is their behavior prompted out of a desire to be a good citizen, or its it the fear of lawsuits or the attractiveness of tax breaks that guides their actions?
- How does the company treat its customers? Are they sincerely interested in the customers' welfare, or are hidden agendas operating?

Your task is to compare the answers to these questions with your own set of values. Ultimately, it is the fit between them that will determine the success of the match.

GET TO KNOW YOUR BOSS

It won't matter how hard you work or how much success you have with the tasks assigned if those things are not important to your supervisor. Likewise, your efforts will produce little success in the organization if your supervisor doesn't like the way you do things or the way you approach him or her. In the article "Managing Your Boss," Gabarro and Kotter advise, "You are not going to change either your basic personality structure or that of your boss. But you can become aware of what it is about you that impedes or facilitates working with your boss and, with that awareness, take actions that make the relationship more effective."[3]

It is important to realize that when managers talk about "managing your boss" they are not referring to manipulation, maneuvering, co-opting, or other devious ways to get the boss to do your bidding. Not at all. Gabarro and Kotter write, "We are using the term to mean the process of consciously working with your superior to obtain the best possible results for you, your boss, and the company."[4] You may feel that it is not your responsibility to "manage your boss," but you must ask yourself the question, "Whose job is it?" If you wish to succeed and to get promoted, it is your job, whether you like it or not. Learn to respond to the needs that your supervisor has. You were hired because he or she thought you could help. If you don't know what is important to your supervisor, how can you help?

---

[2] Gary A. Cluff, "Understanding Corporate Culture," *Journal of Career Planning and Employment* 48, no. 3 (March 1988): 46.

[3] J. J. Gabarro and J. P. Kotter, "Managing Your Boss," *People: Managing Your Most Important Asset* (Boston: Harvard Business Review, 1987): 5.

[4] Ibid., p. 1.

DEFINE YOUR JOB AND YOUR ROLE

In order to be helpful to your supervisor, and enhance your opportunity for promotion as well, know what your supervisor expects of you. Job dissatisfaction commonly results from a conflict between the supervisor's expectations and the employee's assumptions of what the supervisor wanted.

Discuss your job and its responsibilities with your supervisor. Try to understand what he or she wants and whether you have the ability to fulfill those expectations. At the same time, you should make your needs and expectations known to your supervisor. In other words, you must define what Gabarro and Kotter call *mutual expectations:* "Developing a workable set of mutual expectations also requires that you communicate your own expectations to the boss, find out if they are realistic, and influence the boss to accept the ones that are important to you."[5]

In many organizations today, performance evaluations are based on a set of goals to which the employee and supervisor have agreed. If this is the case in your organization, be sure that the goals are clear, measurable, and achievable. Your goals should reflect the priorities of the unit, your supervisor, and you. Too often an employee accomplishes an excellent set of objectives, only to find that those tasks were not important to the organization or to the supervisor. In Sections 3 and 4 you were given specific suggestions for writing performance objectives and for using them in evaluations.

TAKE ACTION

During your cooperative education/internship assignment, did you ever observe that an employee had terrific ideas but never seemed able to carry them out? This situation occurs frequently. There are those who can formulate very clear and original ideas but can never translate those thoughts into action. Most employees are not hired to be *just* idea men or women. In order to get ahead, employees must put good ideas into practice. This does not imply that you, as the newest employee, must make earth-shattering changes in the products or services of your organization. What it does suggest is this: when you have the opportunity to observe a problem, use that opportunity to put into practice an idea that you feel might work. Be a risk taker—as long as you have thought about your course of action and its probable consequences.

The next thing to remember about taking action is always to exceed the job requirements and your supervisor's expectations. You will enhance your position by doing more than the minimum for satisfactory performance. Someone whose efforts are always satisfactory but never superior does not get promoted very often. Excel and don't worry about who gets the credit. Again, unlike your experience in college, the unit performance counts, not that of the individual. This doesn't mean that you should not make your contribution known, but make it known to your supervisor, not to everyone else in the organization.

This is perhaps a good time to point out that not all assignments are going to be of great excitement or interest to you, as you may already have discovered. Remember the opening quote in this activity: "Winners have learned to do things that losers do not want to do." Performing well on those menial and uninteresting tasks will eventually get you some interesting ones. Winners do well at all tasks and even volunteer for some of the menial ones. As the newest employee, you must "pay your dues." After all, the organization and your supervisor need to know what it is that you can do. You are being tested, so be patient and do your best.

Activity 11 suggests that you volunteer for tasks. Many supervisors believe that you enhance your position by assuming greater and broader responsibilities. Be careful that you don't take on too much and allow your other tasks to suffer. However, when your boss wants someone to take a particular assignment, don't be afraid to let him or her know that you are available. Another time, when a more attractive special assignment comes along, you will have the reputation of being ready, willing, and able.

Whenever you take action, remember to be dependable and honest. It is easy to volunteer for a task, but then you must see it through. To leave work unfinished and make excuses is sure to have

---

[5] Ibid., p. 8.

a detrimental effect on your career. Gabarro and Kotter warn, "Few things are more disabling to a boss than a subordinate on whom he cannot depend, whose work he cannot trust. Almost no one is intentionally undependable, but many managers are inadvertently so because of oversight or uncertainty about the boss's priorities."[6] Whatever you do, be dependable. If something goes wrong, or the task is one that you discover you cannot handle, be honest about it with your supervisor. You will earn more respect this way than by looking for excuses or scapegoats.

Although you should not worry about who gets the credit when a unit's task is successfully completed, you do need to make your supervisor aware of your contribution to the total effort. This point underscores the importance of maintaining good communications with your boss. In order to be promoted, your contribution must be recognized. Letting your work be known is just part of establishing your professional credibility. In *How You Really Get Hired,* John LaFevre says, "A new employee's credibility rating is established within six months of employment." He identifies three factors in establishing credibility: "(1) completing tasks on schedule; (2) following through on all commitments; and (3) [having] competence acknowledged by peers and supervisors."[7] It is the third point that concerns recognition. If your work is thorough, accurate, and consistent, your co-workers and supervisors will know. Your best advertising is the quality of your work; let it speak for you. If you disagree with your boss, or your boss's assessment of your performance, it is counterproductive to blame your poor rating on his or her lack of ability in evaluating your work. The boss you must satisfy first is the boss you have today. This is the person who controls your access to promotions.

TAKE CARE OF YOUR SUBORDINATES

If you are responsible for directing the work of others, take care of their needs as well as your own. The supervisor who ignores the needs of subordinates will not succeed in the long run. The unit might perform well in the short term, and its success might even be attributed to leadership and good management. In the long run, however, a team will begin to fall apart if there is no cohesiveness binding it together. Cohesiveness comes not from fear of your reprimands but from a desire to work for you. Human relations are important for job success. You cannot succeed in moving up in the organization if everyone dislikes you. This means that you must be a problem solver, not a problem creator. The members of your team must be able to turn to you for assistance when they are having difficulty. If you can offer only additional problems, they will stop coming to you as the manager they can trust.

DON'T FORGET THE CUSTOMER

In the final analysis, it is the satisfaction of your customers or clients that may determine how fast you progress in your organization. Your internal campaign will let your supervisors know what you can do; it is equally important to let the service you give your clients speak for you. A series of customer complaints to your supervisor will assuredly harm your image. Conversely, having clients who occasionally compliment your service is a sure way of getting favorable attention. You are not, of course, advised to solicit praise from clients. If they are happy, it will be evident. Never lose sight of whom it is you serve.

CONTROL YOUR CAREER

At the beginning of this activity the importance of taking control of your career was mentioned. Since it is *your* career, you need to take steps to move in the direction you have chosen. One of the most important aspects of controlling your career is the area of communications. The importance of good oral and written skills cannot be overstressed. Nothing will destroy your promotional opportunities faster than the inability to speak in public and to write so that you can be understood.

---

[6] Ibid., p. 9.
[7] John L. LaFevre, *How You Really Get Hired* (Englewood Cliffs, N.J.: Prentice-Hall, 1986).

The business world is full of memos, letters, sales reports, technical reports, and surveys. What good are these necessary documents if they don't communicate?

Regardless of your major field of study in college, it is imperative that you work continuously on your writing and speaking. Preparing reports and presenting them effectively will gain you recognition faster than almost anything else. A good written and oral presentation can do much for a mediocre performance, but a poor presentation will not help a good performance. You publicize your competence through the way you use words.

There are ways in which you can develop your writing style. Writing courses are available through local two-year and four-year colleges. Workbooks and writing institutes can help. Use a style that is appropriate to the situation and choose words that help the reader visualize your meaning. Your goal is to produce a reaction from your reader that obtains positive results. Reaction and results are paramount in getting promoted. Don't let shortcomings in this area retard your progress.

Your behavior is also a critical factor in controlling your career. LaFevre says, "You must take an active stance in controlling your own career path. If you simply keep your head down and your nose to the grindstone, the only thing that will occur is the removal of your nose. Hardworking employees are appreciated, but not necessarily promoted."[8] He offers several recommendations:

- Do your own work first, then look for ways to help co-workers.
- Be socially active in the company.
- Develop your own education plan each year.
- Be active in professional associations.
- Become active in the community.
- Develop clearly defined career goals.

Are you ready to take control of your career? It is too important to leave in someone else's hands. Consider the suggestions in this activity in light of your past employers and your career to date. Are there some things that need work? Make a list of the steps you should take to ensure that your present position will lead to a promotion.

1.

2.

3.

4.

5.

6.

7.

8.

---

[8] Ibid.

ACTIVITY 22
Understanding the Nature and Economics of the Job Market

Purpose: To describe the changing nature of the job market and its impact on future employment. To consider the implications these changes have on your staying employed.

Depending on whose analysis you read, you can conclude that the changes occurring in the labor market either will produce a "boom" in employment during the period surrounding the year 2000 or will result in "doom." These boom-or-doom projections are especially confusing since economists themselves differ on the matter. There are those like John Naisbitt (*Megatrends*) who feel that, only if armed with an understanding of the coming changes, can one prepare now to acquire skills necessary for future employment. Others, like Dr. Ravi Batra (*The Great Depression of 1990*), claim that a depression surpassing that of the 1930s in scope is unavoidable. Whatever happens, one thing is certain already: the workforce of the year 2000 will be quite different from that of the present or of any other time in our history.

A few quotes from the government report *Workforce 2000: Work and Workers for the 21st Century* are particularly revealing: "The new jobs in service industries will demand much higher skill levels than the jobs of today. . . . Ironically, the demographic trends in the workforce, coupled with the higher skill requirements, will lead to both higher and lower unemployment; more joblessness among the least skilled and less among the most educationally advantaged."[1] Activity 26 discusses the need for an educated workforce, but the idea of importance here is that those who do continue their education and who are flexible in the job market will continue to be employed. The same report also states that U.S. manufacturing will be a much smaller share of the economy in the year 2000 than it is today. Service industries will create all of the new jobs and most of the new wealth over the next 13 years. Whereas some predictions claim that there will, in fact, be some new jobs created in manufacturing, most economists agree that the total increase will be negligible.

What does all this mean to the man or woman graduating from college today? It means that the nature of work is changing. In an article in *Training and Development Journal* on "The Future of Jobs, Work, and Careers," the authors observe, "Jobs flow from work, but not all of the work of a nation has to be finalized into economic-based job contracts. This is why a nation can have a lot of work to complete but may have few jobs. . . . Careers flow from jobs. As implied earlier, a job need not lead anywhere; it is just something a person gets paid for." The authors describe a career as "primarily the invention of large corporations and government bureaucracies." Of great concern is their statement that "the notion of a career as the very centerpiece of the good life is beginning to disappear."[2] If we accept their view of a career, it is obvious that spending many years doing the same thing or working for the same organization is no longer realistic. Movement and flexibility are the answer.

---

[1] *Workforce 2000: Work and Workers for the 21st Century* (Washington, D.C.: U.S. Government Printing Office, 1987): xiii.

[2] J. L. Leach and B. J. Chakiris, "The Future of Jobs, Work, and Careers," *Training and Development Journal* 48, no. 4 (April 1988): 48.

CHANGING DEMOGRAPHICS AND THEIR IMPACT ON THE JOB MARKET

In his "Excerpts from *The New Demographic Realities for Education and Work*," Harold Hodgkinson mentioned a number of demographic trends that will have an impact on the lives of today's college graduates. Among them are the out-migration of youth from many states, the increase in the numbers of workers of black and Hispanic origin, an aging white middle class, and an increase in the number of Asian–Americans. Of particular note is his examination of the kinds of jobs being produced by our changing economy. Occupations that have had the greatest *percentage increase* from 1970 to 1980 include these: data processing machine mechanics, paralegals, computer systems analysts, office machine operators, computer programmers, and aero-astronautical engineers. Remember, though, these are occupations that did not exist a few years ago, so their rapid growth is measured against a very low base number. Look instead at the occupations that employ the most people and you get a very different picture. The leaders in *numbers* of new jobs are janitors, nurses' aides, salesclerks, cashiers, waiters and waitresses, general clerks, food preparation specialists, secretaries, and truckdrivers. These are low-pay, low-skill, part-time or temporary jobs with few benefits and little chance for advancement.[3]

For the college graduate, the picture seems considerably brighter. As the number of less-skilled workers increases, the need for managers and administrators also increases. The movement to a more technologically oriented workforce requires that the demand for technical graduates and for business graduates will continue to be strong. As our teaching force ages and the "baby boomers" have children, there will be an increased demand for elementary school teachers. Other kinds of teachers, especially those with special-needs training or interest in the daycare industry, will find ample employment. The same can be said for most health care occupations, particularly those requiring college degrees.

One of the phenomena of our times is the sudden and increased interest in the liberal arts graduate. The Boston newsletter of the Bureau of Labor Statistics said, "The ideal job candidate may well be the liberal arts major with technical electives who has maintained a good grade point average and has participated in a co-op program or has some other related work experience."[4] Since the bureau estimates that the average worker will change jobs six times in his or her lifetime (others have placed the number of changes at from five to twenty), it may be that the liberal arts background provides the broadest level of skill development and problem-solving ability without the narrower focus of a technical or business degree.

Do you know what the fastest growing occupations are nationally or in your immediate area? Go to your library or career resource center and locate some of the statistical reports on occupational outlook. Publications such as *The Occupational Outlook Handbook* and *The Occupational Outlook Quarterly* and reports from the Bureau of Labor Statistics and the Division of Employment Security will be especially helpful. In the space provided, list the ten fastest-growing occupations requiring a college degree.

1.

2.

3.

4.

5.

6.

7.

8.

---

[3] Harold L. Hodgkinson, "Excerpts from *The New Demographic Realities for Education and Work*." (Paper presented at the Alden Seminar, February 14, 1985.)

[4] U.S. Bureau of Labor Statistics, "Outlook for College Graduates in New England," *BLS News* (May 29, 1988): 2.

9.

10.

Do you have some level of transferable skill in any of these occupations? What impact does this information have on you? Have you considered other skill training? Where was your "ideal" occupation on the list? Are there areas of skill training, not at the college level, that would be of additional interest to you?

Don't overlook secondary occupations. People sometimes live rewarding lives by combining an underutilized specialty with some other skill. Adults who have degrees in music and play the violin might supplement their income by building and restoring violins. Others in the music field perform in orchestras when possible, but may work as computer operators. There are archaeologists who sell neckties and teachers who supplement their income as furniture makers. In the future, secondary occupations could become an important source of income, thereby allowing people to continue in low-paying occupations that they enjoy.

Even those graduates with technical degrees may have difficulty finding the job they want in certain geographic areas or in their specialties. In recent years, the entrepreneurial sector of the high-tech industry has been advertised as "today's gold mine." Yet graduates seeking employment in this sector have found difficulty in locating entry-level positions. Eileen Wilson, in the *Journal of Career Planning and Employment,* suggests that these jobs are "not as readily available to entry-level technical college graduates as current reports would lead us to believe."[5] She suggests gaining early exposure to these occupations and giving careful thought to curriculum planning as two possible solutions. An editorial in the same journal points out that "whole layers of middle management have been wiped out by corporations in their quest for a lean and mean posture."[6] In the future, a career may not necessarily progress through the ranks of middle management to top executive.

ECONOMICS OF THE JOB MARKET

The important aspect of this discussion is its emphasis on understanding the nature of the job market. In his article "The Economics of the Job Market," Jack Shingleton says, "Knowing the job market and one's marketability can be a big help in finding a satisfying and rewarding job."[7] Such topics as supply/demand ratio for college graduates, current salary ranges and future trends, inflation and its impact on the value of the dollar, the differences in the job market in different geographic regions, and the projections of employment in different fields are all considerations when looking at your potential in the labor market. The more information you have, the better you can prepare to meet the challenges of the future.

Labor Market Supply and Demand

Shingleton says: "One of the best indicators of the future is what has happened in the past. The supply/demand ratio for college graduates is no exception to this rule. Even with today's rapid changes in the field of employment, job candidates would do well to rely, at least partially, on what has happened in the past, since there has been a fairly constant supply/demand curve in the various disciplines throughout the past decade."[8] One of the recognized leaders in career planning and placement, Shingleton knows what he is talking about. For the past seventeen years, his office at Michigan State University has published a study entitled *Recruiting Trends.* So what does his study show at present? "Generally speaking, students in the technical areas, sciences, accounting, and business, and the medical fields have found a ready market for their services upon graduation;

[5] Eileen Wilson, "The Expanding High-Tech Job Market: Myth or Reality?" *Journal of Career Planning and Employment* 48, no. 2 (January 1988): 49.

[6] *Journal of Career Planning and Employment* 48, no. 2 (January 1988): 2.

[7] Jack Shingleton, "The Economics of the Job Market," *CPC Annual* (Bethlehem, Pa.: College Placement Council, 1987): 33.

[8] Ibid., p. 33.

but there have been temporary pockets where supply exceeded demand—for geologists, for example.''[9]

Shingleton also mentions that a bachelor's degree with a master's in some specialization can be an excellent combination. Here are some majors that have more jobs than candidates:

- Business and management
- Computer and information sciences
- Engineering
- Health professions

Fields in which the number of jobs equals the number of candidates available include

- Mathematics
- Physical science
- Agriculture
- Architecture and environmental design
- Education
- Library science

The professions in which the supply of graduates exceeds the number of jobs available include

- Biological Science
- Communications
- Fine & applied arts
- Foreign languages
- Home economics
- Natural resources
- Psychology
- Public affairs
- Social Sciences

These projections agree very closely with those of the Division of Employment Security and the Bureau of Labor Statistics.

Rising Salaries and the Real-Dollar Value

''An important indicator of the supply/demand ratio for graduates is the diverse range of salary offers apparent from one major to another,'' says Shingleton.[10] The salary statistics in his report present an entry-level range of approximately $15,000 from the lowest paid to the highest paid major.

Shingleton makes a further significant point: ''The real-dollar value of a college degree in many majors has eroded during the past ten years. This erosion is more marked in the low-demand areas—home economics, communications arts, and the social sciences—than in engineering. In most disciplines, the average salary paid in real-dollars is less today than 10 years ago.''[11] Whereas the Consumer Price Index has increased about 6.7 percent per year during that period, average salaries have increased from 4.0 percent (for social science majors) to 7.9 percent per year (for computer science majors) over the same period. Shingleton offers these suggestions: ''People in low-demand areas must think in terms of working harder to find jobs in their fields of study. Second, if they don't finds jobs in their field of study, they should consider alternative careers. Third, they should consider accepting jobs in their fields of study even though they might be underemployed, with the hope that when higher level vacancies occur, they will be able to move into those positions.''[12]

---

[9] Ibid., p. 33.
[10] Ibid., p. 33.
[11] Ibid., p. 34.
[12] Ibid., p. 34.

Go back to the list you prepared at the beginning of this activity. Was your desired occupation on the list of fastest-growing occupations? Was it in the group that has more jobs than applicants? Was it in the group that has just enough jobs, or was your career field one of those that is experiencing an oversupply of graduates? Your college's career resource center or placement office or the reference room of your library provides sources of career information. Locate some of those references and answer these questions.

How has the real-dollar value of salaries in your discipline changed in the past ten years? Has it kept pace with the increase in the cost of living?

Importance of the Academic Institution and Experience

Two important factors that recruiters consider when looking for college graduates in a tight labor market are the reputation of your institution and the kind of experiences you have had. Shingleton notes, "The quality of an institution from which a person graduates has always made a big difference in the employment opportunities available. Moreover, until some better criteria is found, the grade point average will continue to be one of the main measuring sticks used by employers in the hiring process." This reminder emphasizes the need to do your very best in each course, regardless of whether or not you like the course or instructor. Your past performance is still a good indicator of future performance.

The fact that you have participated in a cooperative education/internship program means that you have already answered the second point—experience. Use that experience to its fullest. Not every graduate can demonstrate competence in the skill areas that you have practiced. More than skill development, you have acquired work habits that have been evaluated. You have an established work ethic and have paid some of the dues along the way. Each of these factors gives you an edge in the competitive world of employment.

Geographic Differences

When researching the demand for workers by field and by salary, you may have noticed that demand varies from place to place. In *Megatrends,* John Naisbitt pointed out that there are definitive shifts in employment according to geography. He even named specific cities that would grow and others that would decline. The Bureau of Labor Statistics and *Recruiting Trends 1987–1988* affirm that fact. According to *Recruiting Trends,* "the regions of the United States in order of best availability of jobs are southwestern, northeastern, southeastern, northcentral, southcentral, and northwestern," in that order.[13]

In order to be employed in the future labor market, one must be geographically mobile. Inevitably, personal preferences for areas of residence become secondary concerns. A greater problem still is increasing family dependence on two incomes, which means that a move entails finding new jobs for both partners.

---

[13] Jack D. Shingleton and L. P. Sheetz, *Recruiting Trends 1987–88* (East Lansing, Mich.: Michigan State University): 8.

STAYING EMPLOYED IN A CHANGING ECONOMY

So far, this activity has outlined the problems inherent in a changing labor market. This final section and some of the activities that follow point to some solutions.

Both career seekers and career development professionals must change their view of career development. Until recently, career development professionals have emphasized what Leach and Chakiris refer to as the **Linear career form,** defined as "the traditional corporate or government career ladder model." These authors suggest that we need to consider two other models as well: the **free-form career** and the **mixed-form career.** The free-form career "includes work for pay and work or activity for no pay. . . . These activities are free form in nature because they aren't structured within a corporate organization chart."[14] Sometimes employees "lease themselves out" to other firms or start small businesses in their spare time. Personal autonomy is one characteristic of this form of career plan.

The mixed-form career is based on "the notion of behavioral transitions," according to Leach and Chakiris. "Mixed-form careerists are making significant changes in their repertoire of skills, knowledge, and attitude orientations as these bear upon their work."[15] In other words, there will be movement between linear and free-form patterns at various times in one's life.

Putting the matter in another light, Jeffrey Hallett, in his article "The Changing Face of Work," states that "the social contract between employers and employees will be radically different in the future." He continues, "It is this very basic idea of a predictable 25- to 30-year career as the ideal employment arrangement for both employee and employer that has shaped the role and function of education, organization, and management in this country. Unfortunately, that idea no longer holds and, therefore, neither do the institutions, practices, and agreements that were created to support that earlier reality."[16] This is one of the major concerns for the future employee. Since organizations are less likely to be able to predict their future needs with any degree of certainty, the graduate, to stay employed, must constantly be looking for the next job. Career and job changing, a suspect practice in the past, will become necessary in the future.

More than ever before, employees will need to stay abreast of current trends and attuned to what various organizations are doing in the labor market. Reports such as the *Fortune 500* lists and *Business Week*'s Global 1000 lists will become required reading for tomorrow's employee. Mergers, buy-outs, takeovers, and so forth will need to be studied with care. It will be informed employees who stay employed, provided that they have learned to identify transferable skills and can market themselves.

In order to keep pace with these changes and to prepare for movement, the wise graduate will need to continue his or her education. Education will become a lifelong activity; the degree will not be enough. Members of many professions and professional organizations are already required to obtain a number of continuing education credits each year in order to maintain credentials. This trend will continue and become part of each graduate's necessary portfolio.

To recapitulate, be mobile and learn to maximize the advantages you possess. Your skills, your training, your experience, your flexibility, your willingness to change jobs for the same employer (or to change jobs to another employer), and your willingness even to change careers will all be essential. Some graduates have had seven or eight jobs in as many states during thirty years of employment, while others have stayed with a single employer for that same period of time. Rare is the graduate who has been with one employer for thirty years, but has changed jobs seven times and had four or five different careers while with the same employer. Be aware that this pattern has been the exception in the past but could become commonplace before the end of the present century.

---

[14] Leach and Chakiris, "The Future of Jobs," p. 52.

[15] Ibid., p. 52.

[16] Jeffrey J. Hallett, "The Changing Face of Work," *Journal of Career Planning and Employment* 48, no. 2 (January 1988): 53.

Understanding the Nature and Economics of the Job Market

ACTIVITY 23
Expanding Your Educational Horizons

Purpose: To help you discover further opportunities for education in your chosen field and other kinds of training that might be of interest.

Why do young graduates decide to attend graduate school or further their education? The answer may be simple for some, complex for others. In an exciting article, "The Enrollment Crisis That Never Happened: How the Job Market Overcame Demographics," Paul Harrington, of the Center for Labor Market Studies, points out that "over 75 percent of entering freshmen at private institutions said getting a better job was a very important reason for going to college."[1] This reason is also one of the major ones for continuing with graduate school. More education in this country has always meant upward mobility.

Harrington gives us a clue to another reason that motivates students: "Rapid growth in the service industries generated a large number of jobs, which in turn caused the ratio of new jobs in the professional, managerial, and technical occupations to new college graduates to rise sharply."[2] One of the reasons that recent college graduates pursue additional training is to seek positions as managers. Another strong motivator for graduate training is promotion to a management position. Third, further education has always been viewed as synonymous with higher pay. Finally, there are many who just wish to pursue an academic discipline without regard to its consequences for employment. Each of these reasons is sufficient to make graduate school attractive.

For the holder of an associate's degree, the opportunity to obtain a bachelor's degree in the interests of job security and upward mobility is a similar motivator. Many of the reasons cited above apply to this group as well. In addition, some career fields change their requirements over time. For example, in some states the associate's degree or the three-year diploma was until recently the accepted credential for nursing practice, just as it was thirty years ago. In many states the accepted credential has now become the bachelor's degree. Nurses with an associate's degree or nursing diploma are returning to school in large numbers to obtain bachelor's degrees in order to remain competitive in the labor market. This same scenario has been played out in other professions as well.

There are other ways of continuing education besides graduate education, and many college graduates are enrolling in a large variety of programs and courses. During the teacher surplus, many teachers who lost their jobs through cutbacks returned to school to acquire new skills as computer operators, social workers, secretaries, and office managers. A simple desire to acquire new skills is one reason that people continue their education. The more options you have, the less likely you are to be unemployed for long periods of time.

Others go back to school to acquire or hone skills that were not sufficiently mastered in their degree program. Managers seek to improve their human relations or writing skills. Professionals in all fields take courses to acquire computer literacy. Businessmen and women with the potential for

---

[1] Paul E. Harrington, "The Enrollment Crisis That Never Happened: How the Job Market Overcame Demographics," *The Chronicle of Higher Education* (April 8, 1987): 11.

[2] Ibid., p. 11.

overseas assignments need to acquire language proficiency. Teachers of English or social studies may desire to enhance their employment opportunities by becoming math teachers. Elementary teachers who wish to teach special-needs students may seek additional certification. Every year, many professionals return to the classroom to improve their reading comprehension and reading speed in order to stay current with the volume of professional literature that crosses their desks daily.

Employers responding to the question "What skills do you look for in potential employees?" generally include computer literacy, problem solving, basic writing, basic reading, basic math, and English as a second language for employees for whom English is not their primary language. Many employers provide courses at the job sites, absorb a share of tuition expenses, or completely underwrite the cost of continuing education. The larger corporations have extensive training departments to handle specific kinds of training, such as skill training and managerial development. Some corporations even operate their own degree-granting institutions. In Massachusetts, for example, A. D. Little offers a master's degree in management, Wang has a graduate school, and Massachusetts General Hospital is licensed by the Board of Higher Education to grant both bachelor's and master's degrees in certain disciplines.

GRADUATE SCHOOL PLANS

You may now see many reasons why graduate school could be important to you. The decision to pursue graduate education, though, should be carefully considered. It is difficult and time consuming, and it requires a great deal of personal effort and commitment. In return, there must be a payoff for you. Answering the following questions should help you to assess whether attending graduate school should be in your plan.

1. Is a graduate degree required for progress in your chosen field?

2. Look around you. Do most of the workers who have been in the profession for a few years have advanced degrees?

3. Do you have the stamina and ability to complete a graduate degree?

4. What institutions offer the degree programs you might pursue?

5. What are the approximate costs?

6. How might they be financed?

7. Is there some sort of reimbursement policy at your organization? What are the restrictions?

8. When should you start to realize the benefit of your investment?

9. Can you pursue your graduate training on a part-time basis? Is this a desirable option?

10. Is a doctorate degree required for success?

11. What kinds of degrees do the top executives possess?

In her article for the *CPC Annual,* Elinor Workman cites the following reasons why students choose graduate school: it is required for entry into certain professions, such as law and medicine; it is something they really want to do; or they are unsure of their career goals and want to "find themselves." She points out that some fields require an academic degree and others prefer a professional degree. Her strong recommendation is that you do further research "on the programs best suited to your interests and goals." Further, she says, "As you evaluate each program, consider such factors as: the quality of the faculty, the prestige of the institution, the facilities, the overall cost, placement opportunities, housing, geographic location, surrounding community, and any other factors of personal importance." Examine the ratings on each graduate school, but, she cautions, "read the introduction of each rating carefully to see how judgments were made."[3] Each rater uses different criteria for rating graduate schools. Be sure you know the basis for the particular rating you are reading.

OTHER EDUCATION AND TRAINING

Not all employers and professions require advanced degrees, and many of them require other kinds of training regardless of whether the employee has an advanced degree. Training is one of industry's highest costs, but it is a necessary one. What kinds of training might you consider?

---

[3] Elinor Workman, "Graduate School in Your Plans?" *CPC Annual* (Bethlehem, Pa.: College Placement Council, 1987): 61.

Continuing Education Credits

Many professions, particularly in the health care fields, now require that a professional acquire certain continuing education credits each year for renewal of the license. It may be up to you to choose where you go to obtain those credits and what specific kinds of training you pursue. Consider, therefore, what sort of training will do the most for your career. More important, be sure that you earn the required number of credits each year. Don't take the chance of losing your license.

Skill Training or Management Training

Whether to seek additional skills training or to move into the management area is another decision you will have to make. No one can make it for you. Again, consider your career goals and values. Do you want to be a manager? Do you have the personal characteristics it takes to be an effective manager?

State-of-the-Art Courses

Some professions change so rapidly that professionals must take "state of the art" courses on a regular basis in order to keep abreast of current developments in the field. Engineering and computer science are typical of fields affected by this requirement. Many courses, seminars, and even video courses via telecommunications systems may be available at your place of business or nearby. If you wish to progress in your profession, you need the training that keeps you on the cutting edge. It is immaterial who pays for the course. It is to your advantage if your organization pays, but your continued professional development requires it anyway. Once again, consider your career development needs.

Career Development Seminars

Some people need training in career development issues themselves. When it comes time to make a change, you may need to seek help with résumé writing, interviewing, or job search strategies. The person who remains employed will be the one who has up-to-date skills and knows how to market himself or herself. It is in this latter area that career development seminars may help. The training, personnel, and human resource management departments in many corporations now offer various services to employees in the area of career development. Corporations recognize the cost involved in replacing workers who leave and have developed counseling services to assist with job changes within the organization. Internal job change is a way of retaining workers who are mismatched·in their current jobs but still valuable contributors to the organization.

1. If your organization has a training department, what kinds of training programs does it offer?

    a. Who may attend?

    b. When are the training sessions held?

c. What benefits seem to result from attendance?

2. If your organization does not have a training department, where do employees go to get required training? Who pays the cost?

3. What kinds of training are advisable for you?

4. What is rewarded more in your organization, skill training or management training? Which is of greater interest to you?

5. Are continuing education certificates awarded?

6. Does your profession require a certain number of continuing credits each year to continue your license?

7. Is continuing education important for your career development?

Many companies, professional associations, colleges, and training institutes offer a wide variety of workshops and seminars that might be of interest to you. As a professional, you may receive brochures and flyers on many such resources in the mail each week. Some kinds of training will be required or strongly suggested by your employer, who will expect to pay for it. Other kinds of training might be of interest to you and your career advancement, but will not be reimbursed. Some expenses for training should be a part of every professional's personal budget. Without professional growth, you cannot expect to succeed.

Recreational and Leisure Courses

It would be inappropriate to end this activity without saying something about education and training that is not directly tied to your job or career. Many professionals today find that their productivity can be enhanced by renewing their energies in non–work-related activities. Consider the account executive who is an avid sailor on the weekends, or the engineer who paints landscapes. There are college professors who find that working with their hands allows their mind to rest and become renewed. These activities may require some skill training and development. Courses of this nature can be fun and can lead to a better, more complete lifestyle. For some, hobbies can lead to supplemental income and/or retirement occupations.

Employers recognize that the employee who can relax and renew himself or herself in weekend and evening diversions is a happier and more productive employee. Are you already involved in leisure activities or do you need to develop some?

1. What are your hobbies?

2. Realizing that you may not have had time to develop many hobbies while attending school, ask yourself what you like to do with your leisure time.

3. If money were no object, what would you do when not working, such as on vacations and weekends?

4. What kinds of training would assist you in developing your interests? Where is such training available?

Develop a plan for the use of leisure time. This undertaking requires attention as careful as the thought you devoted to developing your career interests. Activity 15 presented ways of relieving stress. Your leisure pursuits can do much to dispel the effects of job stressors. You should see an improvement in your productivity after "getting away from it all." It is important to your career development and to your employer's evaluation of your performance.

ACTIVITY 24
Networking and References

Purpose: To describe networking and how it can assist you in your job search. To examine the use of references.

Probably the best job search technique available is that of networking. In career development and career planning circles, networking is the technique most often discussed in recent years. In his book *The Complete Job Search Handbook,* Howard Figler writes, "People more often find their work through direct referral by other people—usually friends or acquaintances—than in any other way." He describes a **network** in these terms: "Acquiring employment is a social process. People are connected to one another by a nearly infinite number of pathways. Many of these pathways are available to you, but you must activate the circuits to make them work to your advantage."[1] This process is referred to as **networking.**

Eli Djeddah maintains that networking allows you to "enter the unpublished section of the job market, which covers 80 percent of the jobs available to you." He continues, "Your purpose in the unpublished section of the market changes drastically. It is no longer to get an interview. Your highest objective now is to make a deeply favorable impression on the people you call on . . . those who can give you the job you really want."[2]

WHAT IS NETWORKING?

Think about your previous jobs, whether part-time or summer employment. How often did that job result from knowing someone who knew someone, who knew someone else? This was no chance happening but an organized campaign to get you the job you were seeking. You may not have thought of it as organized, but it was not as haphazard as you may suppose. Regardless of your lack of experience or the few employers you have had, you still have valuable contacts. This is the beginning of your network. The goal of networking is to be referred by your contact to other contacts at higher levels in organizations or at the level you need to reach to become employed. You really want a job, but you only ask for advice. Everyone wants to be asked for advice, and people willingly give it to those who have made a favorable impression on them. They can't help it. Their egos are involved. If a job can be found in the organization, very well. If not, it is in the executive's best interest to refer such a good candidate to someone else, who will be grateful.

There is a difference between networking and mentoring. A network contact is just that, a contact. A mentor is more than just a contact. A **mentor** is a person who not only provides contacts but also offers guidance and counsel. **Mentoring** is a process that involves the mentor and the person being mentored over a long period of time; it requires the building of a long-term relationship. Mentors can be an excellent source of contacts. Your mentors could be the appropriate beginning for your network.

---

[1] Howard Figler, *The Complete Job Search Handbook* (New York: Holt, Rinehart & Winston, 1987): 121.
[2] Eli Djeddah, *Moving Up: How to Get High Salaried Jobs* (Berkeley, Calif.: Ten Speed Press, 1971): 72.

Most people can look back over their lives and identify an individual or two who have been mentors. Perhaps it was a relative, friend, a neighbor, a Scout leader, a member of the clergy, or a teacher. List one or two people who were mentors to you as you were growing and developing.

1.

2.

You have just started building your network list.

HOW DOES NETWORKING FUNCTION?

There are four steps to the networking process: making your list, refining it, using it, and starting to network. Begin by listing the names of friends, neighbors, parents of friends, former employers, people you worked with in civic, church, or social groups, and anyone else you can think of who might be in a position to know someone you wish to know. Figler is unequivocal about it: "There is no such thing as a person who cannot be contacted, reached, tapped, exploited, or otherwise made a friend."[3]

Some people, Djeddah included, would suggest that you make several lists, according to how relevant each contact is. However you approach the task, the list is the key to networking. In making your list, don't forget professional organizations, sports teams on which you participated, clubs you belonged to, people you met through hobbies and interests, and any celebrities you may have met.

A source of leads available at many schools is the alumni network. In recent years, many placement offices have been developing alumni career networks with the cooperation of their alumni offices. It may be that your institution already has such a network in place. Talk to your career counselor and find out. If not, you could be instrumental in helping to start one, and at the same time gain valuable contacts. Remember, as an alumnus of your institution, you are now a member of a very special club. Alumni have been assisting alumni for hundreds of years. These alumni networks do not just operate in the halls of Harvard, Yale, and the rest of the Ivy League. Each school has its own loyal alumni who want to assist other alumni of their school. Visit the alumni office and find out what is available to you.

Don't expect to sit down and complete your network list in an hour. Work on it over time. As you conduct your regular business, you will remember people you forgot to list. Add them. Slowly the list will grow. Don't rush your list, and never feel that it is complete. Even if you are not looking for a job, you should maintain your network list. In discussing how to acquire a personal referral network, Figler says, "The best time to look for contacts is when you are not looking for contacts. When you are in a desperate hurry to find the right contact, you will probably turn this person off with your impatience."[4]

Once you have amassed a fairly respectable list, it is time to start refining it. Make notations about each person listed: job, employer, place of residence, leisure activities, and so on. Record any relevant information that you can acquire, including people with whom they might have contact. These notes are the refinements that will be of greatest assistance when you begin to use your list. At this point you can eliminate any person too isolated to help.

Quoted in an interview with M. Opsata, Jack Bilson of Burroughs offers some good advice on when to begin making your networking list: "From the first quarter of your freshman year until you have accepted a job offer in the last quarter of your senior year, you cannot afford to overlook any event that makes company representatives available to you, especially when they come right on campus."[5] This is sound advice. Begin your network list from the first day you enter your institution, or begin right now if you haven't already done so. Before using your list, however, be sure you know what it is you wish to ask each contact. Do you want information on the person's

---

[3] Figler, *The Complete Job Search Handbook,* p. 123.
[4] Ibid., p. 125.
[5] M. Opsata, "The Personal Touch," *Graduating Engineer* (October 1985): 148.

career? a critique of your résumé? help in reviewing your skills? Plan first. Don't bother a contact unless you are prepared and have specific questions. Otherwise you could turn that contact off and effectively eliminate that person from your list.

Some final reminders on networking. Be sure to keep the members of your network informed on what you are doing. An occasional note will suffice. Some people have maintained network contacts over many years. Even if retired, those contacts are still interested in the career progress of their younger colleagues and still have contacts of their own. Many faculty members keep detailed records of former students and continue to provide networking services to those who keep in touch. Former students are also part of the faculty member's network.

Last, don't forget to thank those people who provide networking services for you. After making your contact, take the time to write a brief and sincere thank-you note. Your thoughtfulness and courtesy will solidify the relationship.

The following questions are designed to assist you in starting your personal career network. The names you list are the beginning of a network that will constantly expand as you make additional contacts.

Who Can Help Build My Career Network?

1. Which relatives?

   a. Mother, father

   b. Sisters, brothers

   c. Aunts, uncles

   d. Others

2. Which neighbors?

   a. Those I know

   b. Those my parents know

3. Which school contacts can help?

   a. Classmates

   b. Sorority sisters/fraternity brothers

   c. Teachers

   d. Other university personnel

   e. Alumni

4. Who can help me from my previous employment?

   a. Employers

   b. Co-workers

   c. Customers

   d. Others

5. Who can help me from leisure and volunteer contacts?

   a. Clergy

   b. Club members

   c. Fellow hobbyists

   d. Sporting contacts

   e. Former teachers

   f. Friends

   g. Former coaches

   h. People from civic organizations

6. Who are the other professionals that can help?

   a. Family doctor, dentist

b. Bankers, insurance agents

c. Lawyers

d. Others

Highlight with a marker those contacts who you think would be good ones to help you begin expanding your networking list. Try to choose two or three contacts from each category. When you contact these people, ask them to give you additional names—people who would know something about the kinds of jobs you are seeking. Add those contacts to your list and keep expanding it.

For other similar activities designed to get you thinking about networking, see those at the end of Part 2 of *The Complete Job Search Handbook,* by Howard Figler.

SELECTION OF REFERENCES

The purpose of references in the employment process is to afford the prospective employer the opportunity to talk to people who know you, so that assertions made on your résumé and in your cover letter can be verified. This is the minimum benefit from a reference. A person serving as reference might actually volunteer to call and sell your qualifications to a prospective employer and could become involved in providing you with additional leads and/or contacts. In other words, the person providing you with a reference should be part of your network—a very special part.

Who makes a good reference? Many of the people whose names appear on your network list. However, the person serving as your reference should know you well and should have had contact with you in some specific capacity. Former employers make good references, as do former professors, counselors, co-op coordinators, internship coordinators, advisors to college organizations, and other professionals. In addition to considering their specific professional background, you want to seek out people who feel positive about you and who can write well.

In general it is recommended that you have three lists of references: employment references, academic references, and personal references. Anyone who can speak about you as an employee, about your work habits, and about your job performance is a potential employment reference. Those who can discuss your academic ability and academic performance can serve as an academic reference. Individuals who can discuss you as a person, your character, and your personal attributes are those whom you should seek as personal references. A good recommendation is that you have six to nine names, including some from each category (but not identified as such), typed on a piece of paper with addresses and phone numbers, ready to be left with anyone who requests a list of references.

It is helpful if the sources of reference are those who can address the needs of each employer. Therefore, you might wish to indicate to a prospective employer which of the references on your list would be the most appropriate to contact. Try to avoid having nonspecific, general recommendations sent to those employers who request references. "To whom it may concern" letters, although helpful in a placement file in the placement office and relatively easy to write, do little to provide specific information to the prospective employer. When possible, encourage the employer to telephone your references directly, thus allowing your reference providers to be of maximum assistance. For those positions you really want, ask your reference providers to write specific recommendations. Supply them with not only a copy of your latest résumé but a copy of the job description so they can tailor their comments accordingly. It is those specific references that will be of the greatest help to you.

Finally, don't forget to be sure that you have permission to use the names of each of those serving as references. This means contacting them in advance, providing them with a copy of your résumé, and keeping in touch as you progress with your job search. Try to avoid asking the same person repeatedly for specific recommendations. The longer your list, the less frequently you should have to call on the same person for the favor. Be sure, also, to select those people as references who are dependable and who will provide letters when requested. The most impressive name as a reference is no good to you if that person procrastinates when asked to supply you with a reference.

It seems unnecessary to mention that you should select only people who will make positive comments about you. Each year, however, teachers, employers, and peers are asked to provide references for former students, former employees, or former colleagues about whom they can say nothing positive. It is always surprising when a person fails to recognize the unlikelihood of receiving a positive reference. Apparently some people are not astute about their relations with others. If in doubt, ask the reference provider if he or she feels comfortable in recommending you to a prospective employer. You will get an honest answer.

In the space provided, list individuals (with names, addresses, and phone numbers) who you feel could serve as your references.

Academic References:

1. Name _____

   Title _____

   Address _____

   City, state, zip _____

   Phone number(s) _____

2. Name _____

   Title _____

   Address _____

   City, state, zip _____

   Phone number(s) _____

3. Name _____

   Title _____

   Address _____

   City, state, zip _____

   Phone number(s) _____

Employment References:

1. Name _____

   Title _____

   Address _____

   City, state, zip _____

   Phone number(s) _____

2. Name _____

   Title _____

   Address _____

   City, state, zip _____

   Phone number(s) _____

3. Name _____

   Title _____

   Address _____

   City, state, zip _____

   Phone number(s) _____

Personal References:

1. Name _____

   Title _____

   Address _____

   City, state, zip _____

   Phone number(s) _____

2. Name _____

   Title _____

   Address _____

   City, state, zip _____

   Phone number(s) _____

3. Name _____

   Title _____

   Address _____

   City, state, zip _____

   Phone number(s) _____

When you have completed this exercise, type these names, addresses, and phone numbers in two columns on one side of a single sheet of paper under the heading "References." Make copies for placement with your résumés since there is usually insufficient space on the résumé to list specific references. Do not include this list automatically when sending out or handing résumés to prospective employers, but have copies available for those who request it.

ACTIVITY 25
Changing Jobs

Purpose: To help you understand the reasons why people change jobs. To help you prepare to make a job change.

There are countless reasons why people change jobs. The Bureau of Labor Statistics estimates that more than 6 percent of the workforce available each month is unemployed. The actual percentage may be even higher, since there are many unemployed who for various reasons are not part of this statistic. Bolles reports, ''During a typical year, some 20% of the total work force find themselves out of a job—one out of every five workers.'' The reasons he cites are underemployment, work dissatisfaction, burnout, job turnover, and career change.[1]

Whatever the reason, the toll that job change takes on the individual is enormous. It affects one's attitude, lifestyle, and self-esteem. Many people who are unemployed change their behavior in such a way that it seriously impairs their ability to find another job. Their attitude toward work changes. Most serious, though, is the impact that unemployment has on one's self-esteem. No one likes to admit to being unemployed. It raises too many questions about one's competence, or so many people think. Being deprived of steady income for a long period of time also affects one's lifestyle. Together, the impact of these changes can be devastating.

Much of the stress that affects workers comes from rapid changes in the business world. But these changes are out of the control of the individual worker. Today's business environment produces change in the workplace more suddenly and more frequently than ever before. Mergers, acquisitions, hostile takeovers, deregulation, new technology, and organizations going through cycles of centralization and decentralization are all factors that contribute to job uncertainty. In previous activities, you have learned that job change in the future will almost certainly become more frequent, rather than less so, and that most workers can expect to change jobs and even careers several times during their working lives.

The phenomenon of frequent job change is now being referred to as **career transition.** This term apparently gives the idea of job changing some respectability. Studies conducted by career development specialists, by professional journals, and by a variety of government agencies suggest that people entering the workforce today will have more than ten different jobs and perhaps as many as six different careers in their lifetimes. The average job may last less than four years. Job change will become the rule rather than the exception.

REASONS FOR CHANGING JOBS

What makes people anxious about changing jobs? Why do they tend to resist change? Even when a career change would be a favorable move, many people hesitate. The following exercise should help you explore your feelings about changing jobs.

Imagine that you have been working after graduation for nearly a year in a job with which you are satisfied. Suddenly, and without warning, the company you work for is taken over by a larger

---

[1] R. N. Bolles, ''Your Career: The Basic Principles of Life/Work Planning as They Apply Particularly to the World of Work, Job Hunting, and Career Change,'' *Success Life/Work Planning Guide* (Chicago: Success Unlimited, n.d.).

organization, which decides to trim the labor force. You have been notified that your position is being eliminated and that in two weeks you will be unemployed.

1. List the worst things that could happen to you if you remained unemployed for six months.

2. Now look at each item on your list. What could you do to lessen the impact of each one of these problems separately? Address each issue as if it were the only one.

3. What scares you the most about the prospects of being unemployed?

4. What could you do to survive for six months without a job?

Addressing concerns before they occur and developing alternative courses of action alleviate some of the anxiety surrounding job change or unemployment. You should always be thinking about your next job and making plans. It has been said that the best time to look for a job is when you have one. There is much truth in that statement. Don't wait until you are unemployed to search for other options than what you are now doing. Spend some time each year fantasizing about the kinds of jobs that you might try if you were not employed in your current position.

In coming to terms with your situation when unemployed, it makes a big difference if your termination was voluntary or involuntary. There is little stigma attached to the individual who decides, for personal reasons, to leave one job and seek another opportunity. Unless you are unemployed for a long period of time during that process, it seems quite natural to make changes that will benefit your career. If you are terminated involuntarily (fired), the reason for your termination becomes very important. On the one hand, loss of a job due to the organization's consolidation or retrenchment of positions for cost containment or planned shrinkage is less likely to be viewed unfavorably by a prospective employer. On the other hand, if your termination was prompted by your alleged inability to fulfill your job responsibilities, then you have a different problem when seeking new employment. You will need to demonstrate your ability to perform and communicate your level of competence despite your previous employer's evaluation. Meeting this challenge will require careful planning.

Of course, the major reason for voluntary job changes is upward mobility. Occasionally, however, a lateral change is desirable when a similar and equal position is more to your liking and will produce greater satisfaction, especially a position that is closer to your field of interest or involves a skill that you wish to develop.

As the large number of "baby boomers" moves through the labor market, a new pattern of movement is developing—not upward or sideways, but downward. Why would anyone move down in an organization? In many cases, the reason is job satisfaction. Take, for example, the engineer who decides that he or she wants to be a manager and competes successfully for a managerial position. After some time in the position, the person concludes that management is not what he or she thought it would be. Doesn't it make sense for this dissatisfied person to admit that the management position was a disappointment and go back to being a good engineer?

Career counselors are now recommending a step down on the career ladder in a large number of cases involving employee dissatisfaction. Do the things you like to do. It is not viewed negatively when a college administrator decides to return to classroom teaching. Why should it be viewed negatively when corporate managers decide that they would like to return to their own professional fields? Lawrence J. Peter, in his book *The Peter Principle,* explained that people tend to get promoted until they reach their level of incompetence. Once they reach that level they tend to stay there, unpromotable, unhappy, blocking any opportunity for a competent person to fill that job. He asks if it would not be better to allow that person to drop back to his or her highest level of competence. Although his book is to some degree a tongue-in-cheek approach to management problems, it contains much wisdom. Today career counselors are putting his suggestion into practice.

Whatever kind of job change you make, upward, downward, or sideways, be sure that, for you, it is a change for the better. Don't change simply for the sake of changing. Change to make some aspect of your life better and more fulfilling. Second, realize that your values and personality will evolve as you grow and mature and have new experiences. As you fulfill some of your life's goals, others will become more important to you. Some of these goals might require great changes in your lifestyle and work style. Consider very carefully your reasons for changing, weigh the advantages and disadvantages, and devise a plan for action.

There is something to be gained from experiencing crises in life, although those benefits may be lost from view during the time of crisis. Each crisis that one survives makes one less fearful of the next crisis and better able to cope. In the body of literature written regarding change, particularly organizational change, it is suggested that, without a sense of crisis, change would not occur. This principle probably applies to individuals as well. If your life is going along happily and without problems, why change? What would be the motivation to do so? It is only when something is not right that a person attempts corrective action. That crisis builds a commitment to change, without which change will not happen.

SKILLS NEEDED TO CHANGE JOBS SUCCESSFULLY

Once you realize that change is inevitable, you can develop skills to make change less threatening. Having alternate courses of action is important as well. This exercise examines how that approach might work.

1. Please list three different changes that have taken place in your life during the past year.

   a.

   b.

   c.

2. What impact did these changes have on your lifestyle and/or plans for the future?

   a.

   b.

   c.

3. What courses of action could you have taken that would have altered the outcome of each event?

   a.

   b.

c.

4. Describe, in general, what further changes would have occurred in your life if you had taken a different course of action on any of those events.

In planning a job change, the first thing you need to do is to analyze what you have to offer to prospective employers. You have done this to get your first job, but now the attention to transferable skills becomes even more important, especially if you decide that a change in direction is warranted. Transferable skills have a certain timelessness about them. If you were good at problem-solving in elementary school, then you are probably still good at problem-solving today. Once acquired, skills do not disappear from your repertoire just because you have not used them recently. They may need to be sharpened somewhat, but you still have them. Like riding a bicycle, they're something you never forget.

The next step is to determine what the marketplace wants. Howard Figler has suggestions, noting that some skills are more important to employers than others, even though all skills have value. Figler describes his "ten hottest transferable skills" as those that are universally greeted with enthusiasm because they are needed with some regularity in every job having responsibility and requiring decision making and good judgment. This is his list:[2]

- Budget management
- Supervising
- Public relations
- Coping with deadline pressure
- Negotiating/arbitrating
- Speaking
- Writing
- Organizing/managing/coordinating
- Interviewing
- Teaching/instructing

Look back at the list of skills you developed in Activity 1. How many of the "ten hottest" do you have? Figler says, "If you cultivate any three or four of these skills to a high order of proficiency, you are doing quite well. If you practice most of them and feel you are improving in each, you should expect to have positions of decision-making and responsibility before long." Remember, though, you need to assess what you have first and then see where your skills fit on this list.

How would you rate your ability on Figler's "ten hottest" list? Place a check mark in the columns to indicate your self-rating for each skill.

---

[2] Howard Figler, *The Complete Job Search Handbook* (New York: Holt, Rinehart & Winston, 1987).

Skill	Terrible	Average	Good	Very Strong
Budget management				
Supervising				
Public relations				
Coping with deadline pressure				
Negotiating/arbitrating				
Speaking				
Writing				
Organizing/managing/coordinating				
Interviewing				
Teaching/instructing				

Having decided what skills you have (and determined that there is a need for those skills), you need to communicate that fact to prospective employers. Regardless of the reason for your job change, you must present yourself as seeking the change for your own good. LaFevre says, "Career changers must always present themselves as being in complete control of their career development. Don't ever describe a career change as due to an external factor outside your control. Companies only hire candidates who are in control of their own destinies."[3]

Project a positive image. One of the reasons that chronically unemployed professionals cannot find work is that they have begun to describe their plight in terms of the negative impact that someone or something had on their lives. In other words, they either blame someone else for the situation or fault events over which they had no control. They often make such negative statements as, "I would have been all right if. . . ."

During a period of job change, be patient and persistent. Job changes seldom come easily, nor do they happen overnight. It is easy to become discouraged if the first several contacts do not prove fruitful. Keep working at your job search and analyze your performance to be sure that you are not missing something. It may take time, but your career is worth the effort. Likewise, don't grab at the first job offer that comes along. Be sure it's one that you want. Be selective.

Identify your sources of support. During this time, you will need people who can be understanding and helpful. Support can come from many different people with whom you have regular contact. Sources of support may be parents, friends, mentors, teachers, counselors, members of the clergy, advisors, roommates, or significant others—anyone whom you feel is helpful when you have a personal problem. Making use of your support systems and support groups will assist you in keeping your perspective and in developing a healthy attitude toward your situation.

When making any kind of job or career change, you should examine all the options available to you. This means that your thinking should not be constrained by your immediate past. Imagine that you were unemployed today and could do anything you wished (except live like a millionaire without working). What are some of the things you've always wanted to do? Here is your chance to fantasize a bit. List five or six things you always wanted to do in your lifetime or in fantasy.

1.

2.

3.

4.

---

[3] John L. LaFevre, *How You Really Get Hired* (Englewood Cliffs, N.J.: Prentice-Hall, 1986).

5.

6.

Pick one of the items from your list and write a paragraph describing what factors are preventing you from doing it and what you would need to do or have in order to live out this fantasy.

Recognize your options, no matter how remote they seem, and explore whether any of them offers possibilities that you might be overlooking now. The loss of a job can be a great source of trauma in your life or a great source of opportunity. This could be your big chance.

When you are changing jobs, your career network becomes more important to you than ever before. That is why Activity 24 suggested that you continue developing your network list, even if you are not looking for a job. You never know when you will make a contact that could mean a new job or career option for you. Now is the time to bring your network list up to date and to start using it. More than ever, you need access to that unpublished job market, which you can reach only through your career network. Remember, 80 percent of the jobs available are never made public.

LIFE/CAREER PLANNING

When it becomes necessary to change jobs, it is time to do some serious life and career planning. Perhaps your former career plans are no longer relevant. Maybe your lifestyle has changed or your goals have shifted somewhat. Don't just look for another job doing what you've been doing for the past few years. Use this opportunity to assess where you are in your life and where you want to be. Life/career planning can be viewed as a six-step process:

1. Self-assessment
2. Skills identification
3. Career awareness
4. Decision making
5. Goal setting
6. Job finding (preparing résumés, interviewing, and so forth)

This book has led you through all of them. You should automatically retrace these steps for yourself at this time.

Now is the time to broaden your options for the rest of your life. A narrowing of specialization is likely to lead to unemployment in the future. What is needed today are generalists who can continue to learn and to grow and who are flexible enough to move in new and exciting directions. Can you change directions? Do you want to? These are the questions that deserve answers when you consider a job change.

Peaks and valleys occur in the course of everyone's life. The patterns of highs and lows in your career could suggest directions that are appropriate for you. There are many exercises that help you look back over your life to date and chart or graph events as high points and low ones. Bolles' article or Hagberg and Leider's 1982 *The Inventurers* or similar publications in your library or career resource center suggest several ways of doing this. Try one of these activities when you are considering job changing. Move *with* your strength and *to* your strength.

ACTIVITY 26
Developing Your Personal
Marketing Plan

Purpose: To use the information you have developed about yourself and your career field to prepare a personal marketing plan.

During your progress through this book, you have been collecting information about yourself (your likes and dislikes, your abilities and interests) and the realities of the job market (what jobs are available, what skills are needed). Now it is time to put all this together, couple it with your work experience as a cooperative education/internship student, and use the information to get the job you are seeking. The way you use this information is called your **personal marketing plan**—for in reality that's exactly what it is. You must market yourself and your abilities to employers.

In the world of marketing there are four *P*s—product, place, price, and promotion. The product is *you*. You must have a saleable product; otherwise, the best price and the best promotion will not help. You cannot sell something that customers don't want. The first step, then, is to look at your product.

KNOW YOUR PRODUCT

You have already assessed your capabilities, skills, and experiences earlier in this book. Now you should examine your skills in terms of your areas of greatest strength. If you were marketing some other product, you would try to capitalize on your product's strengths in the market. Marketing yourself is no different. Go back to the list of skills you developed in Activity 1, your résumé in Activity 6, and the discussion of job descriptions in Activity 13. Keep in mind the requirements stated on the job description and determine your major strengths for a particular job. What is it that makes you unique in the large universe of candidates for this job? Use the outline that follows to prepare your plan for each specific position.

Pick a job description at random from those that interest you. Examine it carefully, as Activity 13 instructed. List the five or six most important items that this employer is seeking.

1.

2.

3.

4.

5.

6.

Next, examine your skills, experiences, and your own résumé. What do you possess that should excite this employer? Name five or six of your qualities that address the employer's needs, as you have just listed them.

1.

2.

3.

4.

5.

6.

These are your areas of strength for this job. In order for this information to assist you, you must maximize the advantage. You cannot assume that the employer will recognize these strengths from your credentials alone. Your presentation will need to emphasize your strengths and direct the employer's attention to them. How to do this is the subject of the section about promotion.

Examining your product was the easy part. The next part is much more difficult. If you were an employer interviewing you, what would stand out as your most obvious weaknesses? If an employer asked, "What are your greatest weaknesses?"—a favorite question of some interviewers— what would you identify? List two or three of your obvious weaknesses in light of this same job description.

1.

2.

3.

OK! So you have some weaknesses. So what? Nobody's perfect. What can you say to the employer that minimizes the impact of these shortcomings? Remember to use the suggestions in Activity 6 on how to provide a superior point to counter objections. In the following space, write a brief answer to questions about each of the weaknesses you cited.

Being prepared in advance to address weaknesses will lessen the fear of discussing them. Perhaps your weaknesses won't be noticed, and you won't be asked. That's all right, but it is better to be prepared. Your answer may not only satisfy the employer but show that you have given some thought to the matter.

One of the questions often asked during the interview is, "How would ——— describe you if I called him or her?" The person named could be a former employer, a former teacher, one of your references, or anyone else who might know you. Imagine that you were that person, and try to describe *you* as he or she would. In the space below, write a paragraph describing yourself as seen by someone else.

POSITION YOURSELF IN THE MARKET

The second *P* in marketing is place. This refers to where you are (your place in the market) and where you wish to be (your market position). Right now, before you begin your job search campaign, "place" means where you are in comparison to all the other candidates who might be competing with you for some job that you want. Are you in the upper 10 percent of likely candidates? Perhaps the upper 25 percent or the upper 50 percent? If you are only in the upper 50 percent, your chances of getting this job are equal to your chances of not getting it. You need to improve the odds.

Where would you like to be in the group of applicants for this position? The upper 10 percent? Here you would have nine chances in ten to be the successful applicant. Is this realistic? You need to identify where you would like to be in order to have a reasonable chance of success, and then develop a plan to get there. What advantages could you present to the employer that other candidates for the same job could not? Look back at the list of strengths you developed earlier. What strengths would you have in common with other applicants? What strengths do you have that most of the other applicants would lack? This is where your work experiences should help you stand out from the crowd. But you also must focus on specific strengths, making them obvious to the employer. Unless these strengths are communicated at the first contact—in your letter of application, cover letter, or the first few minutes of an on-campus recruitment interview—you may not progress any further in the employment process. Follow up after an interview by emphasizing these strengths in your thank-you letter. Consider very carefully what you have demonstrated you can do during the work experience part of your program. This will be your major advantage in developing your marketing position.

Employers who have not had experience with cooperative education/internship students are surprised by these graduates' specific experiences, level of maturity, professional manner, and understanding of the employer's needs. You have more than your skill development in the content areas to impress an employer. You have also developed a whole set of affective skills that make you more employable than those without experience. You know how to deal with a wide variety of co-workers, with people of different ages and abilities, with issues that arise in the workplace, with the relationships that develop or do not develop between fellow workers, and with the whole interpersonal dimension of employment. Advertise these skills.

CONSIDER SALARY AND BENEFITS

Price (or salary) and benefits are usually major considerations in any job search. Your response to questions regarding your knowledge of salary and benefit information will indicate a certain level of maturity and realism. In order to evaluate an offer, you should have some idea of the salary range in the industry in which you are seeking employment. You need to be aware of what the typical or average company or organization is offering, as well as what industry leaders are paying. This information is readily available in several places on campus. In your institution's career resources center or placement office, look for the College Placement Council's annual wage survey. In it you will find average salary offers and median salary offers for various majors. You will also find figures showing average salary offers for each major by type of industry, which are especially helpful. The survey is published in January and March, during the college recruiting season, and in July and September, at the end of the recruiting season. The preceding year's survey provides some indication as to what should be offered in the current year.

Other salary survey information may be available in your library. Many trade publications publish average salary information. Don't forget to ask your cooperative education/internship program coordinator. He or she can probably provide guidance, as could your co-op/internship employer.

The salary offered is only part of an organization's total compensation package. Before comparing job offers in financial terms, be sure you know what benefits each organization is offering. A sharp difference in the benefit package could make a lower salary offer the more attractive one. Certain benefits are standard across an industry, such as group life insurance and medical coverage. Others, though, such as tuition benefits, incentive plans, and the like can differ greatly from one employer to another. Be sure you are not comparing apples and oranges.

PROMOTE YOURSELF IN THE MARKETPLACE

The final *P* in marketing stands for promotion. How do you take the advantages that your product (you) has to offer at your price (salary) and make the package attractive to prospective customers (employers)? Just as you would market any other product, you must begin by advertising. Your letters of application or cover letters that accompany résumés to prospective employers are your advertising media. Activity 7 discussed letters and Activity 6, résumés. Be aware that the form and professionalism that you employ in this process tell the employer something about you as a person. A hastily written letter, not typed and not in correct business form, communicates lack of professional responsibility. Letters and résumés that are obviously thrown together convey a lack of real interest in the job.

Often résumés and applications are received with attached cover letters that are handwritten, or hastily prepared, or so general that the applicant could be applying for any of several hundred openings. These applications are not taken seriously. They are put aside as coming from candidates who don't truly care about the position. This is the point exactly. Poorly prepared letters, both in form and in style, communicate a lack of real interest in the job. Get a decent typewriter or access to one, use a new ribbon, and learn to write letters that are job specific. Your letters and your résumé are your advertising. Don't blow your chance now.

In *Marketing Yourself,* the *Catalyst* staff make this important point: "Preparing a résumé without having some idea of your specific job targets is a little like packing for a trip without any idea of where you're going. You'll probably take along some things that you have no need for and leave some important items back at home. If you don't have a job target in mind when you write your résumé, you'll probably include a lot of irrelevant information and leave out many pertinent facts."[1] This is good advice. Your letters and résumé should, if possible, be targeted to the specific job for which you are applying. If you need to have many copies of a résumé printed, then preparing résumés individually may present some problems. However, if there are two or three specific types of position you desire, consider having two or three different résumés available. The use of a word processor is especially helpful for individualizing your résumé for each position. Another piece of advice from the *Catalyst* staff is to use words and phrases that will give your résumé lively and attractive qualities. If possible, use the words and phrases that the employer has used to advertise the position. You could check some of the job descriptions you have obtained and see what words and phrases are most often used.

Armed with clear, stylish, and attractive advertising copy (your résumé and letters), go back to Activity 5 and Activity 24 and bring your list of contacts up to date. Develop your network further, if necessary, and select those contacts that appear to offer the greatest assistance in pursuing the job you are seeking. Use other sources available—newspapers, trade journals, job listings in various places—and decide where you should begin.

Be sure that your presentation—both written and in person—has a flow to it, that it addresses the employer's needs, and that it emphasizes the strengths that make you the best candidate for that particular job. And believe it! A salesperson who doesn't believe in the product will not be successful. Check your written communications and your selection of attire and personal grooming to be sure that each one projects the kind of image you want.

Again, remember that your previous experience will "sell" you if properly presented. Figler says, "Self-marketing is the ultimate transition skill to carry you from one job to the next because it allows you to see links between what you are doing now and the work you will choose tomorrow."[2] Presenting yourself to prospective employers must be deliberate and purposeful. Although there always seems to be an element of haste in the job search effort, you must never make it appear that you are acting hastily. Knowing your transferable skills intimately will allow you to proceed with purpose and direction. Remember, it is how you present your transferable skills that makes you the candidate of choice. Be deliberate in this regard.

---

[1] *Catalyst* staff, *Marketing Yourself: The Catalyst Women's Guide to Successful Résumés and Interviews* (New York: Putnam, 1980): 27.
[2] Howard Figler, *The Complete Job Search Handbook* (New York: Holt, Rinehart & Winston, 1987): 230.

ACTIVITY 27
Evaluating Your Total Program

---

*Purpose: To acquaint you with the purpose of program evalua-
tion and to assist you in evaluating the cooperative education/
internship program that you have just completed.*

In his manual *A Handbook for Evaluating Cooperative Education Programs,* James Wilson describes evaluation as "a process of collecting relevant information, examining and analyzing that
information, interpreting it and making judgments about the program by comparing the interpreted
information with agreed upon standards." Further, he says, "Evaluation results are intended to be
highly individualized as between one situation and another."[1] In essence, then, this will be your
individual interpretation of what you know about the cooperative education/internship program
and its benefits to you.

Of the many types of evaluation—formative, summative, input, discrepancy, secondary, and
transactional—the only one of concern here is the input evaluation. An **input evaluation** provides
information about the necessary and available means to reach the projected program goals. True,
you are looking at your total program at the end in a sort of summative way, but the purpose is to
provide you and your program coordinator with helpful information so that, first, you can add to
your experiences, and second, the program coordinator can devise ways to improve the program.

REVIEWING YOUR PROGRAM

The steps indispensable to the evaluative process are essentially those that John Dewey elaborated
in his classic problem-solving model:

1. Specify the objectives.
2. Identify the elements to be examined.
3. Collect the data.
4. Analyze the data.
5. Interpret the data.
6. Identify the strengths and weakness of the program.

As you examine each of these steps in detail and perform it, you will also be putting the information into a format organized for your final report.

Specify the Objectives

In the first place, you must be clear about both the stated program objectives and those specific
objectives that you hoped to accomplish when you chose to participate in the cooperative educa-
tion/internship program. Think back in time to when you decided to apply for the program. What
were the stated program objectives that attracted you to the program? List them here, using the
catalog or other promotional materials that describe the program.

---

[1] James W. Wilson, *A Handbook for Evaluating Cooperative Education Programs* (Boston: National Commission for
Cooperative Education, 1979): 4–5.

1.

2.

3.

4.

5.

What were your personal reasons for participating in the cooperative education/internship program?

1.

2.

3.

4.

5.

Identify the Elements

What data do you already have regarding the outcomes of your program? Consider such things as periodic employer evaluations of your performance; grades before and after participating in the work experience program; letters of reference and/or contacts made while working; evaluative discussions with your program coordinator; and comments from faculty members regarding your work experience. List the sources of information that you already have to assist you in evaluating your program.

Collect the Data

For a realistic evaluation, you probably need some pieces of data that you do not have but should get before you start. List any other items of information you still need and where you can obtain them. Then go collect this data. For example, do you know how your salary compares with that of the other co-op/internship students in your class and major? This statistical data should be available from your program coordinator.

Data Needed   Where Available

Analyze the Data

The next step in evaluating your program is to analyze the data in terms of the advantages and disadvantages of participation in the cooperative education/internship program. Use concise phrases to describe each one.

Advantages   Disadvantages

Interpret the Data

Look at the advantages and disadvantages you have listed. What is your sense of the balance? Does the scale shift in favor of the advantages or the disadvantages?

Your assessment of the results should not be based simply on the quantity of responses under each column. Specific items may outweigh others because of their qualitative importance to you personally. Maybe you will want to assign a weight to each item, on a scale of from 1 to 10, in order to establish relative value.

Identify Strengths and Weaknesses

Consider the advantages that you saw in the program. What strengths do you feel were of major importance to you?

Major Strengths:

1.

2.

3.

4.

5.

6.

Others:

What do you feel was missing from your program? What were some of the goals you had for participation that were not realized? List these as *concerns*.

Major Concerns:

1.

2.

3.

4.

Others:

In every program, there are some experiences or program characteristics that participants do not find particularly worthwhile or helpful. What were some of the aspects that you feel could have been left out of your program without seriously impairing its operation or success?

Unnecessary Features:

1.

2.

3.

4.

Others:

RECOMMENDATIONS FOR PROGRAM CHANGES

The last step in this evaluation process is to describe the changes, if any, that you would recommend. Remember, the coordinators, the program director, the faculty, and the administrators, as well as the employers will all benefit from helpful, well-thought-out suggestions. Your suggestions could also prove beneficial to fellow students who will follow you in this program. The purpose here is not to lay blame, to seek scapegoats, or to air gripes, but to provide constructive feedback for you and for the program director.

What would you do differently if the operation of the program were up to you?

WHAT DID YOU LEARN?

Now that you have finished your cooperative education/internship program, what did you learn that you can use in the future? Make a list of some of the specific knowledge and skill development that resulted from your participation.

Were any of these learning outcomes ones that you could have acquired simply by staying in school and not participating in the work experience part of the program? If so, which ones?

In addition to the learning outcomes, known as *cognitive* outcomes, certain affective or interpersonal outcomes occur during the work experience. What interpersonal skills do you feel were developed or enhanced by participating in the cooperative education/internship program?

You have now completed the evaluation of your program. In this last activity, you have generated lists of the advantages and disadvantages of the program; those advantages that were most important to you; those things that you think should be added, if possible; those things you would leave out, if possible; and your recommendations for improvement of the program. In addition, you have listed those learnings that you feel would be most useful to you, and you have listed those interpersonal skills that you feel were enhanced by your participation in the program.

One final question: Was it worth it? The authors, along with those responsible for the operation of your cooperative education/internship program, sincerely hope so. To quote Herman Schneider, the founder of the cooperative education program at the University of Cincinnati in 1906, "Judgment based upon experience must supplement theory."[2] Our hope is that your experiences have been the foundation for this kind of judgment in your career field.

ADDITIONAL RESOURCES

Applied Management Sciences. *Cooperative Education—A National Assessment: Executive Summary and Commentary*. Boston: National Commission for Cooperative Education, 1978.

Barbeau, J. E. "A Survey of 1988 Graduates, Northeastern University." Unpublished report, Northeastern University, Boston, 1989.

Batra, Ravi. *The Great Depression of 1990*. New York: Simon & Schuster, 1988.

Bisconti, A. S., and L. C. Solomon. *Job Satisfaction After College: The Graduates' Viewpoint*. Bethlehem, Pa.: CPC Foundation, 1977.

Bolles, R. N. "Your Career: The Basic Principles of Life/Work Planning as They Apply Particularly to the World of Work, Job Hunting, and Career Change." *Success Life/Work Planning Guide*. Chicago: Success Unlimited, n.d.

---

[2] Herman Schneider, "Background of the Cooperative System," *Mechanical Engineering* (July 1935): 418.

Campbell, David. *If You Don't Know Where You're Going, You'll Probably End Up Somewhere Else*. Allen, Tx.: Argus Communications, 1974.

"The Careers 1000." *Business Week Careers* (November, 1987).

Catalyst staff. *Marketing Yourself: The Catalyst Women's Guide to Successful Résumés and Interviews*. New York: Putnam, 1980.

Cluff, Gary A. "Understanding Corporate Culture." *Journal of Career Planning and Employment* 48, no. 3 (March, 1988): 46–48.

Cohen, S., and P. de Oliveira. *Getting the Right Job*. New York: Workman Publishing, 1987.

Dillion, R. D., and P. E. White. "Finding the Job That Fits." *Journal of Career Planning and Employment* 48, no. 3 (March 1988): 61–64.

Djeddah, Eli. *Moving Up: How to Get High Salaried Jobs*. Berkeley, Calif.: Ten Speed Press, 1971.

Documented Employer Benefits from Cooperative Education. Cambridge, Mass.: A. D. Little, 1974.

Fielden, J. S. "What Do You Mean You Don't Like My Style?" *People: Managing Your Most Important Asset*. Boston: Harvard Business Review, 1987, pp. 135–145.

Figler, Howard. *The Complete Job Search Handbook*. New York: Holt, Rinehart & Winston, 1987.

Fiske, M. *Middle Age: The Prime of Life*. New York: Harper & Row, 1979.

Gabarro, J. J., and J. P. Kotter. "Managing Your Boss." *People: Managing Your Most Important Asset*. Boston: Harvard Business Review, 1987, pp. 1–9.

Hagberg, J., and R. Leider. *The Inventurers: Excursions in Life and Career Renewal*. Reading, Mass.: Addison-Wesley, 1982.

Hallett, Jeffrey J. "The Changing Face of Work." *Journal of Career Planning and Employment* 48, no. 2 (January 1988): 52–55.

Harrington, Paul E. "The Enrollment Crisis That Never Happened: How the Job Market Overcame Demographics." *The Chronicle of Higher Education* (April 8, 1987): 14–15.

Harrington, T. F., and A. J. O'Shea. *Guide for Occupational Exploration*. 2d. ed. Circle Pines, Minn.: American Guidance Service, 1984.

Hayes, R. A., and J. H. Travis. *Employer Experience with Cooperative Education*. Detroit: Detroit Institute of Technology, 1976.

Herzberg, Frederick. "One More Time: How Do You Motivate Employees?" *Harvard Business Review* (Special edition, 1987): 26–35.

Hodgkinson, Harold L. "Excerpts from *The New Demographic Realities for Education and Work*." Paper presented at the Alden Seminar, February 14, 1985.

Johnson, Keith. "Your First Position: Springboard or Hurdle?" *CPC Annual*. Bethlehem, Pa.: College Placement Council, 1987.

Kleiman, C. *Women's Networks*. New York: Lippincott & Crowell, 1980.

LaFevre, John L. *How You Really Get Hired*. Englewood Cliffs, N.J.: Prentice-Hall, 1986.

Leach, J. L., and B. J. Chakiris. "The Future of Jobs, Work, and Careers." *Training and Development Journal* 42, no. 4 (April 1988): 48–54.

Leavitt, H. J. *Corporate Pathfinders*. Homewood, Ill.: Dow Jones–Irwin, 1986.

Naisbitt, John. *Megatrends*. New York: Warner Communications, 1982.

Opsata, M. "The Personal Touch." *Graduating Engineer* (October 1985): 147–150.

Osmun, M. "Making The Best Connections." *Business World Women* (Special Issue, 1982), pp. 17, 19.

Scott, C. D., and D. T. Jaffe. "Survive and Thrive in Times of Change." *Training and Development Journal* 42, no. 4 (April 1988): 25–27.

Sheehy, G. *Pathfinders*. New York: Bantam Books, 1981.

Shingleton, Jack D. "The Economics of the Job Market." *College Placement Annual*. Bethlehem, Pa.: College Placement Council, 1987, pp. 33–37.

Shingleton, Jack D., and L. P. Sheetz. *Recruiting Trends 1987–88*. East Lansing, Mich.: Michigan State University, 1987.

Sinnott, P. A. "How to Maintain Your Energy in Mid-Career." *Journal of Career Planning and Employment* 48, no. 3 (March 1988): 30–32.

U.S. Bureau of Labor Statistics. *Occupational Outlook Handbook*. Washington, D.C.: U.S. Department of Labor, 1987.

U.S. Bureau of Labor Statistics. *Occupational Outlook Quarterly*. Washington, D.C.: U.S. Department of Labor.

U.S. Bureau of Labor Statistics. "Outlook for College Graduates in New England." *BLS News*. Boston: U.S. Department of Labor, May 1988.

"Who's Sitting on Top of the World? The Global 1000—The Leaders." *Business Week* (July 18, 1988): 139–186.

Wilkes, M., and C. B. Crosswait. *Professional Development: The Dynamics of Success*. New York: Harcourt Brace Jovanovich, 1981.

Wilson, Eileen. "The Expanding High-Tech Job Market: Myth or Reality?" *Journal of Career Planning and Employment,* 48, no. 2 (January 1988): 47–50.

Wilson, James W. *A Handbook for Evaluating Cooperative Education Programs*. Boston: National Commission for Cooperative Education, 1979.

Workforce 2000: Work and Workers for the 21st Century. Washington, D.C.: U.S. Government Printing Office, 1987.

Workman, Elinor R. "Graduate School in Your Plans?" *College Placement Annual*. Bethlehem, Pa.: College Placement Council, 1987, pp. 61–64.